Learning Disabilities

SUNY Series,
Youth Social Services, Schooling, and Public Policy

Barry Franklin and José R. Rosario

Learning Disabilities
Appropriate Practices for a Diverse Population

Barry Edwards McNamara

STATE UNIVERSITY OF NEW YORK PRESS

Production by Ruth Fisher
Marketing by Patrick Durocher

Published by
State University of New York Press, Albany

©1998 State University of New York

For information, address the State Univesity of New York Press,
State University Plaza, Albany, NY 12246

Library of Congress Cataloging-in-Publication Data

McNamara, Barry E., 1949–
    Learning disabilities : appropriate practices for a diverse
population / Barry Edwards McNamara.
        p.   cm.—(SUNY series, youth social services, schooling, and public
policy)
    Includes bibliographical references (p.   ) and index.
    ISBN 0-7914-3883-X (hardcover : alk. paper).—ISBN 0-7914-3884-8
(pbk. : alk. paper)
    1. Learning disabled children—Education—United States.
2. Children of minorities—Education—United States.   3. Learning
disabled children—United States—Social conditions.   4. Children of
minorities—United States—Social conditions.   5. Learning disabled
children—Services for—United States.   6. Learning disabilities—
United States.   I. Title.   II. Series.
LC4705.M46   1998
371.9'0973—dc21   97-46378
                                                       CIP

10 9 8 7 6 5 4 3 2 1

To Fran, Melissa, and Tracy

CONTENTS

ACKNOWLEDGMENTS

The impetus for this textbook came from my experience at Lehman College of the City University of New York. I was fortunate to work with Dr. Jacqueline Jones, former coordinator of the Graduate Program in Learning Disabilities and currently research scientist at the Educational Testing Services, Princeton, NJ. Her contributions to the initial stages of this text were extremely helpful. Her professionalism and collegiality during our years together at Lehman College will always be valued. During those years, I was the coordinator of the learning disability clinic and was fortunate to work with bright, enthusiastic, hard-working, and caring graduate students who shared their talents with children, adolescents, and adults from culturally and linguistically diverse backgrounds. I learned a great deal from both the graduate students and those who attended the clinic. Dr. Robert Delisle, chair of the Department of Specialized Services in Education at Lehman College, was always supportive of the graduate program in learning disabilities and the learning disabilities clinic. It was due to his strong support that these programs flourished and I thank him. Dr. Kathryn Padovano, dean, Dowling College School of Education, has been extremely supportive of this project, for which I am very grateful.

Priscilla Ross, acting Editor-in-Chief and Associate-Director, State University of New York Press, has been incredibly patient, helpful, and supportive of this work. Her encouragement throughout this project is greatly appreciated. I also want to thank her assistant, Jennie Doling. She was always available to respond to my many questions and concerns, and also provided encouragement and support.

Finally, I want to thank my family. They never wavered in their support, and provided me with continuous reinforcement at every stage of the project. There were times when I wondered if I'd ever complete this book, but they didn't hesitate. That support, encouragement, and belief in this project sustained me. A simple thank you or dedication seems so insignificant in relationship to all they have always done for me. Indeed, I do thank them and dedicate this book to my wife Fran, and our wonderful daughters, Tracy and Melissa, with appreciation and love that transcends mere words.

1

Introduction

Consider the following statistics compiled by Advocates for Children of New York, Inc. in their report entitled "Segregated and Second Rate: 'Special Education' in New York" (1992):

- Statewide statistics reveal the overrepresentation of children of color in segregated special education settings. African-American students represent a disproportionate number of segregated special education placements: they constitute 19.8 percent of the general education population and 34.1 percent of the segregated special education population. Similarly, Latino students comprise only 15.1 percent of the general education population, but represent almost 23 percent of segregated special education placements. Conversely, white students comprise 59.8 percent of general education students and only 41.3 percent of segregated special education placements.

- In New York City, African-American students represent a disproportionate number of special education students, constituting only 38 percent of the general education population and 41 percent of the special education population. In contrast, Latino and white students account for 35 percent and 20 percent, respectively, of the general education population and 34 percent and 19 percent of the special education population.

- Children of color represent a growing number of special education students in New York City. From 1985 to 1990, the number of Latino and African-American males in special education programs jumped 11 percent and 5 percent, respectively. The number of white males in special education programs simultaneously decreased by 14 percent.

- Citywide, African-American and Latino students represent a dispropor-tionate number of the most restrictive special education placements. In 1989–90, African-American and Latino students together comprised over 80 percent of the students in self-contained special education classes and special programs. In contrast, white students represented the single largest group—37.2 percent—of students receiving related services only.

- Available statewide statistics evince the overrepresentation of children of color in segregated—that is, separate—special education placements. Across New York state, African-American students constitute only 19.8 percent of the general education population, but represent 34.1 percent of the segregated special education population. Latino students com-prise only 15.1 percent of the general education population, but simi-larly represent a far greater proportion of segregated special education students—almost 23 percent. In contrast, white students, who consti-tute 59.8 percent of general education students, comprise only 41.3 percent of segregated special education placements. Thus, in heteroge-neous areas of the state, the overrepresentation of children of color in restrictive special education placements suggests a racial resegregation of public schools.

- In New York City, African-American students, unlike their Latino and white counterparts, represent a disproportionately large number of spe-cial education placements. African-American students constitute only 38 percent of the general education population, but make up 41 per-cent of the special education population. Conversely, Latino and white students account for 35 percent and 20 percent, respectively, of the general education population and 34 percent and 19 percent of the special education population. Nevertheless, Latino students may soon constitute a greater, and disproportionate, share of special education students. Between 1990 and 1995, the number of Latino males in special education programs jumped 11 percent, while the number of African-American males in special education programs climbed 5 per-cent. At the same time, the number of white males in special education programs decreased by 14 percent.

It has long been realized that there is an overrepresentation of minority group students in special education. Yet a perusal of the facts alone continue to be startling. If New York City is a microcosm of special education in urban settings, we should be alarmed.

Since the early 60s there has been a rapid growth in the number of students classified as learning disabled. With that growth has been the concern regarding the disproportionate number of students from minority groups. On May 31, 1997, the *New York Times* headline read "Special Education Practices in New York Faulted by U.S.":

> The Federal Government last night warned New York City school officials that they must reduce the disproportionately high number of Black and Hispanic students in special education or face a lawsuit and ultimatley the revocation of tens of millions of dollars in Federal aid. (p.1)

It went on to say that the perception that there was a overrepresentation of minority students was true. It also noted that approiximatley 75 percent of the 120,000 students receiving special education are classified as "learning disabled" or "emotionally handicapped."

An agreement between the board of education and the Office of Civil Rights will address these concerns through a series of corrective measures including staff development and parent training. The article concluded with a statement from a lawyer familiar with the agreement: "The reason this case is important is that it sends a message out to school districts throughout the United States that the issue of minority students in Special Education is not one the Federal government is ignoring." (p.22)

The overrepresentation of minority group students being classified as learning disabled and the inherent problems with the definition and diagnosis of specific learning disabilities require significant changes in traditional special education assessment and instruction. These changes must occur so that we can give appropriate attention to the factors of cultural and linguistic diversity and their impact on how students represent and demonstrate knowledge. There is a critical need to incorporate a sensitivity to issues of diversity into educational assessment, curriculum planning, teacher training, and interactions with parents, especially in large urban areas characterized by cultural and linguistic diversity. The goal is simple: to open the assessment process to an appreciation of the complex interactions of culture and language; to provide practitioners with a variety of instructional approaches that recognize the cultural and linguistic diversity found in students classified as learning disabled; to address issues in teacher preparation and to appreciate the significant role parents play in the education of their child with a learning disability.

Clearly, this discussion will consider the work of individuals who represent a variety of fields such as urban education, anthropology, and literacy, to name a few. However, it is not a text on urban education, nor a text on anthropology. It is a text that is geared for practitioners who are aware of the shortcomings of a traditional view of the field of learning disabilities and need a more coherent approach to the identification and instruction of their students who represent a variety of linguistic and cultural backgrounds. It is a text that will address the needs of Wilson. Wilson was referred to a university-based clinic for an evaluation because his parents and teachers were concerned about his school performance. When he was observed in his second grade classroom he sat in the back row. He tried to pay attention to his teacher, but with a small classroom, thirty-five students, and a "new" teacher this was difficult. This was particularly true when it came to reading instructions, specifically when the teacher presented a "phonics lesson."

Wilson's parents came from Puerto Rico four years earlier and spoke little English. Neither read Spanish or English. His ten-year-old sister struggles in school, but is passing. She attends a university-based reading clinic and appears to be making good progress. On a recently administered standardized achievement test, Wilson scored very low, in the third percentile nationally.

As he sits in the rear of the classroom his teacher continues to provide instructions, but it is lost on Wilson. To compound matters Wilson's teacher is a new immigrant to the United States also, having arrived from Ireland one month prior to the opening of the school year. Her lovely " brogue" is lost on the children who represent a variety of cultures and languages, and find it impossible to undertand her. It becomes even more difficult during "phonics" instruction.

Some school personnel suspect that Wilson has a learning disability, although he is not a native speaker and his "language community" speaks and reads Spanish. The reading teacher feels that he has many of the characteristics of students with learning disabilities that cannot be explained merely because he is not a native speaker. However, most of the school personnel are convinced he's just typical of a child raised in a non-English-speaking environment, and if he's provided with bilingual or ESL (English as a Second Language) instruction, he'll be fine. Meanwhile, he sits in the rear of his classroom, passing the time. His teacher struggles to find ways to make this a productive year for Wilson and his classmates. But nothing seems to work.

What is a Learning Disability?

The term "learning disability" is so general that many employ it as synonymous with learning problems, school failure, and the like. In fact, it refers to a specific diagnostic category.

The classification of *learning disabled* has been referred to as the most heterogeneous of any special education classification. An examination of the definition suggests that this heterogeneity refers more to the wide range of academic deficits found in the population than it does to cultural and linguistic diversity.

In 1968, the National Advisory Committee for the Handicapped in the United States Office of Education proposed the following definition, which later was included in the 1975 Education of All Handicapped Children Act, Public Law 94–142.

The term "Children with Specific Learning Disabilities" applies to those children who have a disorder in one or more of the basic psychological processes involved in understanding or in using language, spoken or written, which may manifest itself in an imperfect ability to listen, speak, read, write, spell, or do mathematical calculations. Such disorders include conditions such as perceptual handicaps, brain injury, minimal brain dysfunction, dyslexia, and developmental aphasia. This term does not include children who have learning problems that are primarily the result of visual, hearing, or motor handicaps, of mental retardation, of emotional disturbance, or of environmental, cultural, or economic disadvantage (Kirk and Chalfant, 1984).

The theoretical definition assumes 1) at least average intellectual capacity; 2) a significant discrepancy between achievement and potential; 3) exclusion of mental retardation, emotional disturbance, sensory impairment, cultural difference, or lack of opportunity to learn as primary factors in the student's learning difficulty, and 4) central nervous system dysfunction as the basis of the difficulty. Given the problematic nature of determining intellectual capacity in students of diverse linguistic and cultural backgrounds and of matching a specific achievement score to intellectual capacity and to classroom instruction, the diagnosis of specific learning disabilities is very often a definition by exclusion.

The integrity of intellectual functioning is a critical element in the definition and diagnosis of specific learning disabilities. Learning disabled individuals must demonstrate, by definition, at least average intellectual ability. Therefore, intellectual ability becomes the yardstick by which the student's acceptable level of academic achievement is calculated. However, the concept of easily definable and quantifiable areas of general intelligence is not without its distracters. Some of the most popular standardized instruments are often argued to be culturally biased and to only provide a minimum reflection of the intellectual ability of minority students (Brown and Campione, 1986; Hilliard, 1987; Jones, 1991; Jones, 1988; Samuda, Krong, Cummins, Pascual-Leone, and Lewis, 1989). When students are representative of a linguistic minority, the task becomes even more difficult. Recurrent questions take the form:

- In what language shall the subject be evaluated?

- Who shall do the evaluation?

- Is a simple translation of the assessment instrument appropriate?

If an interpreter is employed, guidelines must be followed.

Plata (1993) lists those skills necessary for interpreters in Spanish. They are:

1. *Proficiency in the Spanish language.* Non-Hispanics should not be ruled out when this criterion is applied. However, they should be proficient in Spanish, including the ability to speak and understand the pragmatics and nuances of the Spanish language. Interpreters need to relay information to Spanish-speaking parents from a pragmatic perspective (that is, couch information in practical rather than idealistic terms). Spanish-speaking parents' understanding will increase if the information being relayed is anchored to their cultural experiences. Parents' acknowledgment of their understanding of the interpreter's message, thus, is an index of pragmatism (Maya and Fradd, 1990).

In addition, interpreters need to know the nuances of the Spanish language (the slight or delicate variations in meaning of Spanish terms and phrases). For example, the sentence *Mi hijo lucha con sus estudios* could have different English translations, depending on the interpreter's knowledge of Spanish. It could be translated to mean "My son wrestles (physically) with his studies," or "My son tries very hard in his studies," or "My son has difficulty with his studies." Understanding the pragmatics and nuances of the Spanish language is essential to conveying correct information during interactions with Spanish-speaking parents and school personnel.

2. *Familiarity with the Hispanic culture and an understanding of its impact on the total lives of Hispanic individuals.* This would entail being able to interpret cues, being sensitive to others' needs/moods, understanding nonverbal language, and understanding how to meet personal/family needs (Brandenburg-Ayers, 1990). Fradd and Correa (1989) elaborated on this impact by stating that Hispanics' interpretation of and approaches to their experiences and needs are different from those of service providers whose background is not rooted in Hispanic culture.

3. *Knowledge of special education concepts, terminology, administrative procedures, and placement alternatives mandated by the Individuals with Disabilities Education Act (IDEA).*

4. *Willingness to take a secondary role in the referral and placement process.* Interpreters must at all times strive to only relay information, not initiate or change it.

5. *The ability to read and write in English.* These skills are essential because interpreters are asked to (a) assist in administering tests, (b) read special education reports and training material, (c) record students' or parents' responses, and (d) make reports.

6. *The ability to appropriately interact with individuals who are from varying cultural backgrounds, who have varying degrees of training, or who have varying degrees of the understanding process.* This could include administrators, students, psychometrists, human service providers, and individuals in the medical and legal professions.

7. *Trustworthiness and integrity.* Interpreters should be able to be trusted to abide by school rules, to maintain the confidentiality of school records, and to respect the rights of parents, teachers, and students.

In sum, interpreters should possess skills that will assist school personnel in accomplishing activities required by the IDEA, especially (a) scheduling parent-teacher conferences, (b) administering tests, and (c) interpreting during parent-teacher conferences when Individualized Education Programs (IEPs) are formulated.

The potential problems in using interpreters include (a) the difficulty of on-the-spot interpretation, (b) loss of meaning in the interpretation process, (c) provincial meaning of words or concepts, and (d) interpreter's hostile feelings toward monolingual school personnel. (Plata, 1982). The above is applicable to any language/culture with the obvious changes relative to the specific language/culture.

It has been argued that when linguistic differences are a factor in intelligence testing, the intelligence test actually becomes an achievement test, a measure of second language acquisition rather than of general capacity to learn (Nuttall, Landurant, and Goldman, 1984; Mercer, 1983). It then becomes almost impossible to make a determination of intellectual capacity based on standardized instruments. This text will address those alternatives. For example, Howard Gardner has challenged the notion of unitary global intelligence (Gardner, 1983). The Harvard professor of education has defined an intelligence as "the ability to solve problems, or create products, that are valued within one or more cultural settings." Rather than accepting the simple distinction of verbal versus nonverbal abilities, each student is viewed as having the potential to possess one or more intelligences from such domains as linguistic, musical, logical-mathematic, spatial, bodily-kinesthetic, and personal abilities. Gardner not only broadens our ideas of what intelligence is, but his argument is deeply rooted in the individuals' cultural context. Students do not approach the standardized IQ assessment with identical sets of cultural experiences, and these experiential differences have a direct bearing on performance.

The Achievement/Intellectual Functioning Discrepancy

The definition of specific learning disabilities also requires that a significant discrepancy exists between some areas of academic achievement and intellectual potential. However, the degree of discrepancy may vary from state of state, making it possible for a student who takes the same test and achieves the same score in two different states to be classified as having a specific learning disability in one of the states and not the other. This also happens in districts within the same state, where more affluent school districts provide services for students who have smaller discrepancies. This process of establishing a discrepancy between achievement and intellectual performance is determined by tests, administered to students who possess basic differences in experiential backgrounds from the population on whom the instrument was normed. Thus the results of such testing cannot be considered to be an accurate index of achievement or potential (Salvia and Ysseldyke, 1995). This is a critical issue in urban areas in which students who are suspected of having a learning disability may represent a variety of linguistic and experiential backgrounds. Furthermore, inherent in the assessment of academic areas is the assumption that the test items reflect what was actually taught in the classroom. This is probably not the case. The need still exists for assessment instruments that are more curriculum-based. Galagan (1985) has argued that "there is simply no legal requirement and little, if any, legal justification under the EHA (Education for the Handicapped Act) for the ubiquitous use of psychometric and projective instruments in the special education evaluation and placement process" (p. 298). Authentic assessment will be discussed further in the textbook.

A Second Language

Although many students in urban areas are classified as language-learning disabled, significant problems exist in the assessment of specific learning disabilities for students for whom English is not the first or only language learned. It should be determined if such students are truly bilingual (English and the other language are understood and spoken equally well); if the students have learned a first language and English is a second language; if the student has limited english proficiency and no other language.

Fradd and Weismantel (1989) note that there are indicators of learning disabilities that are also behavioral characteristics of students who are learning English:

discrepancy between verbal performance measures on intelligence tests	This discrepancy is predictable because those who are not proficient in the language of the test are often able to complete many of the nonverbal tasks correctly.
academic learning difficulty	Students in the process of learning a new language often experience difficulty with academic concepts and language because these terms and ideas are more abstract, less easily understood and experienced than ideas and terms that communicate social interactions and intents.
language disorders	When second-language learners enter into meaningful communication, their speech often appears as language disorders because of disfluencies that are a natural part of second-language development.
perceptual disorders	Even the ability to perceive and organize information can be distorted when students begin to learn a new language.
social and emotional problems	Students in the process of learning how to function successfully in a new language and culture predictably experience social trauma and emotional problems.
attention and memory problems	When students have few prior experiences on which to relate new information, they may find it difficult to pay attention and to remember.
hyperactivity or hypoactivity; impulsivity	When students have little prior knowledge or experiences on which to base present information, they frequently become restless and inattentive.

Central Nervous System Factors

The assumption of central nervous system dysfunction has become perhaps the least observed component in the diagnosis of specific learning disabilities. Because central nervous system dysfunction is so difficult to demonstrate, specific learning disabilities are often defined by the exclusion of sensory deprivation, mental retardation, emotional disturbance, cultural differences, or economic disadvantage as primary factors in the student's underachievement.

For students from economically depressed urban areas, for students whose acculturation is different from that of the standardization population of the assessment instruments used, for students whose native language is not English, and for those students who have suffered lack of opportunity to learn, the diagnosis of specific learning disabilities *should* be extremely complex process. Ironically, it often appears that these very students are the ones most frequently classified as learning disabled. In fact, it is relatively easy to classify culturally different students in urban areas as learning disabled when evaluators do not consider the appropriate match between student and normative population, and do not consider the sociocultural and instructional factors that, by definition, should preclude such a classification. These considerations will be addressed in this text.

In general, a major problem lies in the attempt to identify an atypical learner who, although assumed to be of at least average intellectual ability and without primary deficits in sensory reception, intellectual capacity, emotional adjustment, cultural and economic factors, does not appear to learn specific types of information in the typical manner. The problem is exacerbated in large and diverse urban areas. In many instances evaluators in such areas are faced with the question, "With what type of error do we feel most comfortable: a false positive, in which large numbers of students may be classified as learning disabled when they are not, or a false negative, in which large numbers of students who truly are learning disabled must go without services?"

A major factor in the preponderance of false positives appears to result from the fact that in many urban school districts students will not receive the support services that may be most helpful to them unless they are classified as having some type of "handicapping condition." Howe and Miramontes (1992) suggest that this is one of the major moral and ethical decision that special educators face. They provide a case to illustrate the point.

> Manual is fifth grader. He is a migrant child and has been in and out of Sky Elementary School over the last several years. This year he is having more difficulty than usual keeping up with schoolwork and is lagging far behind in reading. Mr. Fry, his

teacher, is very concerned. He has taken Manuel's case to the child study team in his school. He explained that Manuel's problems in reading stem from an inability to understand the content, a short attention span, and a seeming lack of motivation. The study team suggested that Mr. Fry give Manual some individualized reading instruction, concentrating on building vocabulary. Mr. Fry tried this, but because of Manuel's absences and the need to attend to the 32 other students in his class, he found it difficult to work with Manuel consistently. Manuel was also beginning to exhibit signs of stress in the classroom by acting out and being aggressive toward classmates. Since there were no special reading services available in the building, Mr. Fry eventually returned to the child study team to seek an official referral for special education testing. The team decided that perhaps this would be the best course of action, since Manuel's academic difficulties could indicate a handicapping condition and since there were no other immediate services to which Manuel could be referred.

Dan Singleton, the resource specialist at Sky, tested Manuel and found that although he did have problems understanding vocabulary, he had no auditory, visual, or memory difficulties. Mr. Singleton felt that rather than having a handicapping condition, Manuel simply lacked practice in reading. Mr. Singleton's hypothesis received support when, by reviewing Manuel's records, he discovered that Manuel had attended 10 schools in his short school career and that the main language services, perhaps because his facility with spoken English masked his limited vocabulary and comprehension.

At the staffing, reports given by other individuals on the committee further supported Mr. Singleton's hypothesis. Manuel's intelligence was determined to be average, and he had no identifiable aural or oral problems, although he was three grade levels behind in math. As the evidence accumulated, it seemed that Manuel's academic problems were not attributable to a handicapping condition. It was also clear, however, that he needed intensive, individual help. This need seemed all the more pressing because Manuel had begun to vent his frustrations in class.

Mr. Singleton has time in his case load and feels sure he can help Manuel if given the chance. However, Manuel cannot be placed in the resource room unless he is found to have a handicapping condition. Because no other special services are available in the building (such as a reading teacher, individual tutoring, etc.), the only option for individualized instruction seems to be the resource room.

This is why it is so critical that the assessment process be undertaken in a sensible, reasonable manner, incorporating an appreciation of the diverse nature of students with learning disabilities.

Overrepresentation of Minority-Group Students

The process one undertakes to identify, classify, and provide appropriate educational services to students with learning disabilities is very complex. Add to this the issues regarding a culturally and linguistically diverse population, and it becomes even more complex. Yet we appear to classify these students with relative ease. Note the statistics provided in the Introduction. Clearly we have no difficulty classifying minority group students. One of the major issues confronting the field of special education, specially students who are classified as having mild disabilities (mildly mentally retarded, emotionally disturbed and learning disabled) is the overrepresentation of minority group students (Pugach and Palinscar, 1995).

A report of the Quality Education for Minorities Project (1990) argued that "no subject is more important to providing quality education for minorities than the restructuring of schools." This restructuring must include a reexamination of the assessment and placement of students into special education programs. In 1985 when approximately 116,000 students were enrolled in special education programs in New York City, a commission on special education was convened. In its final report to Mayor Edward Koch, the commission asserted that "thousands of children are labeled as mildly or, to a lesser degree, moderately handicapped not because they necessarily have a handicapping condition but because regular education programs have not adequately dealt with the educational needs of these children" (Commission on Special Education, 1985). The education of approximately 12.5 percent of the total school enrollment was consuming 23 percent of the entire budget. The commission further state that, "Educators have come increasingly to recognize the need to focus on the classroom and teachers . . . and not just students . . . as the possible source of poor school performance" (p.47). Enormous fiscal resources are expended to design curriculum and hire staff to attempt to "remediate" these identified areas of deficit. Notwithstanding the very real need of some children to receive carefully constructed educational support services, the current focus on deficits, especially in minority populations, stands as a barrier to imaginative curriculum design as well as to expectations of excellence in student and teacher performance. Furthermore, the focus on student deficits has frequently resulted in an overrepresentation of minority students in special education programs for the mentally retarded, learning disabled, and emotionally handicapped (Maheady, Towne, Algozzine, Mercer and Ysseldyke, 1983).

This text will address this issue of overrepresentation by examining the referral process, providing alternatives to traditional assessment procedures, and provide professionals with intervention for students and their parents.

2

The Referral Process

In order to address the overrepresentation of minority-group students in special education, it is crucial to examine the referral process. It is here that the trouble begins. A disproportionate number of African-American and Hispanic students will begin the journey that will eventually result in classification and placement in a special educational setting. Unfortunately, most often the setting will be a more restrictive one—that is, a self-contained special education classroom. This chapter will explore the referral process and offer a number of solutions to the problems faced.

Referrals

In these times of diminishing resources for regular classroom teachers, one way to reduce class size is to refer a child for special educational services. It is not unreasonable for teachers to feel the need to "get help" for students at risk or experiencing difficulty in the regular class setting. I am not suggesting that these students be allowed to fail. Rather, that carefully constructed educational support be provided to children in need, but not necessarily through the traditional special education route of referral to classification to placement. Examination of the number of students referred to special education reveals staggering statistics for urban centers.

A study conducted by Research for Better Schools (1986) noted that the median number of new referrals of twenty-eight large urban school districts was 2,358, with New York City reporting the highest number at 33,855. In New York City, the number of students who are eventually classified as special education is approximately 90 percent (Commission on Special Education, 1985). It seems clear that in New York City the referral is just about a guarantee that the child will be placed in special education. Others have also noted a high referral to classification percentage. Algozzino, Christenson, and Ysseldyke (1982) reported that 75 percent of those referred were eventually classified.

Reasons for Referral

A report from the New York City Commission on Special Education (1985) cites three major reasons for referral: 1) poor academic performance without inappropriate behavior 2) inappropriate behavior without poor academic performance, and 3) both poor academic and inappropriate behavior. Others report that many students were referred by regular classroom teachers because they are "off-task," "inattentive," "destructible," and "unproductive" (Bahr, Fuchs, Stecker, Goodman, and Fuchs, 1988). Teachers are clearly looking to special education for solutions to problems occurring in the regular classroom setting.

A study by Anderson, Cronin, and Miller (1986) examined the reasons for referral in a learning disabled population. Of the 269 students who were eventually classified as learning disabled, the reasons for referral were almost equally divided between academic and behavioral problems with academic problems being slightly higher. They also noted that the majority of referrals were vague and general. They did not assist the referral team in the exploration of a specific problem. Bay and Bryan (1992) also note that a combination of poor academic achievement and poor work-related behaviors, such as those reported by Bahr et al. (1988), is more likely to yield a referral. They suggest that in addition to providing documentation for low academic achievement, observing the student and the teacher in the classroom setting, be added, focusing on specific behaviors, such as attending, involvement, and feedback in order to be more effective in identifying those students who are at risk.

In their study Bay and Bryan (1992) sampled a suburban and an urban school district. It is interesting that they decided to analyze the data from each school district reported. They cite the reason for doing this was that the referral to assistance teams (these will be discussed later in the chapter) were in place in the suburban school that enabled the regular classroom teacher to discuss the child prior to referral. No such teams existed in the urban school district.

Finally, it has been suggested that some teachers refer students as a result of the teacher's own low tolerance for learning difficulties (Algozzone, Christensen, and Ysseldyke, 1982).

Referral by Racial-Ethnic Group

The overrepresentation of culturally and linguistically diverse students in special education has been well documented (Willig, 1986; Chin and Hughes, 1987; Trent and Artiles, 1995). Given the referral to classification percentages discussed above, it is to be expected that the referral rate of culturally and linguistically diverse students would be disproportionately higher than expected. In New York City, for example, it has been reported that African-American children were 50 percent more likely than the white students to be referred for special education during their first and second year of school. And while all students referred were twice as likely to be referred for academic reasons only, African-American students were more likely to be referred for behavioral reasons only.

Gottlieb, Gottlieb, and Trongone (1991) examined the referral pattern for parents and teacher in New York City. Most of the referrals were made by teachers (74.7 percent). Of the 328 teacher referrals, 15.5 percent were white, 42.4 percent were African-American, and 42.1 percent were Hispanic. Their analysis of the data indicated that there is a 95 percent chance that teachers refer African-American or Hispanic students more than white students.

More recently Dr. Harold Dent challenged the African-American psychological community to take renewed leadership in the area of testing (Dent, 1994). He stated:

> Originally, when the learning disabilities (LD) classification came into being, it was an exclusion category. It excluded children whose condition was brought about by socioeconomic conditions or cultural deprivation; but over the years, the exclusionary conditions have been ignored. However, since its entry onto the scene there has been a rapid increase in the use of the LD classification. For example, between 1975 and 1985 there has been a 140% increase in the number of children placed in the LD category across the country, compared to only 16% increase of all other categories in special education. So, it would appear that learning disabilities has become another dumping ground for students who are difficult to teach. (p.7)

Pennan (1995) reports that in recent cases the Department of Education's Office of Civil Rights (OCR) has criticized schools for haphazard referral processes. She notes the following "red flags" may indicate that there is a disproportionate number of culturally and linguistically diverse students in special education programs:

- High proportions of special education students are ethnically diverse.

- High proportions of culturally diverse students within certain special education programs, such as programs for behavioral impairment or mental retardation.

- Students of all races and ethnicities not having equal access to a district's pre-referral intervention program or the same quality of program.

- High number of students from one race or ethnic group being referred for evaluation.

- Reasons given for special education referrals being disproportionate by race or ethnicity.

- Patterns of placement differing by race or ethnicity.

Summary

The number of students referred for special education services in urban settings is staggering. The high percentage of these referrals result in placement in special education settings. More troubling is the high rate of referrals for culturally and linguistically diverse students. The question is not whether these students need carefully constructed educational intervention but do these services have to be provided through a segregated special education delivery system? It appears that regular classroom teachers need to be provided with assistance prior to the point where they feel a referral is necessary. The remainder of this chapter will focus on these prereferral intervention strategies.

PRE-REFERRAL INTERVENTIONS

Garcia and Ortiz (1985) suggest that inappropriate placement of language minority students can be prevental by utilizing a prereferral process. Their eight-step process is outlined below:

Step 1

Is the student experiencing academic difficulty?

No   No problems; process ends

Resources (at all stages)
- Administrators
- Planning time
- Instructional resources
- Mandates

Pre-Referral Interventions
(continued)

- Staff development
- Parents/guardians
- Colleagues
- Consultants
- Related agencies
- Community resources
- Other

Yes

Step 2

Is the curriculum known to be effective for language minority students?

No

- Adapt
- Supplement
- Develop

Yes

Step 3

Has the student's problem been validated?

No

- Inter- and intrasetting
- Intraindividual
- Interindividual
- Interteacher perceptions
- Parental perceptions
- Analysis of work samples and behavior

Yes

Step 4

Is there evidence of systematic efforts to identify the source of difficulty and take corrective action?

No

Teacher	**Evaluation of Instruction**
• Qualifications	• Standards
• Experience	• Ongoing data collection
• "Track record"	• Modification based on
• Teaching style	evaluation
• Expectations	• Staff development
• Perceptions	
• Instructional management	
• Behavior management	

Exposure to Curriculum
- Continuity of exposure
- Domains
- Scope and sequence
- Student's entry level
- Basic skills
- Higher cognitive skills
- Mastery
- Practice

Pre-Referral Interventions
(*continued*)

Yes

Instruction	Student
• Motivate	• Experiential background
• Sequence instruction	
• Teach	• Language proficiency
• Reteach using different approach	
• Teach prerequisite skills	• Cultural characteristics
• Language of instruction	
• Effective teaching behaviors	• Cognitive/ learning styles
• Coordination with other programs	
	• Socioeconomic status
	• Locus of control/attribution
	• Modes of communication
	• Self-concept
	• Motivation

Yes

Step 5

Do student difficulties persist?

No

Problem solving was successful; process ends

Yes

Step 6

Have other programming alternatives been tried?

No

Determine program/placement alternatives

Yes

Step 7

Do difficulties continue in spite of alternative?

No

Student remains in alternative program as appropriate

Yes

Step 8

Referral to special education

There has been an increase in the utilization of prereferral intervention strategies suggesting that recognition of the referral, identification, and classification of students with special education needs is cumbersome and inaccurate. This is equally so for students who are mislabeled learning disabled (Pugach and Johnson, 1989). Moreover, as was noted above, the number of students from urban centers continues to rise at an alarming rate. For these students, collaboration among prereferrals before the option of special education is considered is critical. Prereferral intervention strategies are usually classified as 1) informal, school-based, problem-solving teams, and 2) consultation between the special and regular educator (Pugach and Johnson, 1989).

Graden, Casey, and Christenson (1985) developed a six stage model for prereferral interventions. The first four stages represent the actual prereferral, while the last two stages represent the traditional referral process to determine whether or not special education services are necessary. Their model is presented below.

Stage 1: Request for Consultation

The first step requires the regular classroom teacher to request assistance in problem-solving or intervention for a particular student. While it can be initiated on the building level or more formally though a district committee, the former is favored. It seems that if an ongoing relationship is to exist among all professionals (regular and special) rather than a more informal, building-level approach.

Stage 2: Consultation

During the actual consultation process the classroom teacher and the consultant specify the reason for referral in objective and measurable terms. Once this occurs an action plan is formulated and evaluation measures are put into place. Interventions are implemented and evaluated.

Stage 3: Observation

Observation in the classroom setting is the next stage of this model. The observer (it may be a special educator, a psychologist, or a social worker) describes the curriculum, the tasks, and the demands placed on the student. They also observe the behavior of the teacher, physical arrangement of the classroom, and interactions of the student. Causes and consequences of student behavior are also noted. Based upon this observation the appropriate parties meet and discuss the success or the interventions.

Stage 4: Conference

During the conference a decision is made to continue or modify the intervention plan or refer the child for an evaluation to determine special education eligibility.

Stage 5 and 6: Formal Referral and Formal Program Meeting

For those students who are thought to need special education services, a referred and formal program meeting is scheduled to discuss the findings.

Ponti, Zins, and Graden (1988) note that if a pre-referral process is to be implemented, a number of organizational factors need to be considered. They apply the principles developed by Maher and Bennet (1984) and Maher and Illback (1985). This framework is referred to as DURABLE (Discussing, Understanding, Reinforcing, Acquiring, Building, Learning, and Evaluating.) This approach allows a school to make decisions regarding the effectiveness of a program, whether to modify or eliminate it.

The authors note that the intervention chosen was linked to the needs of the school rather than imposed. This is critical. The needs of students who are culturally and linguistically diverse are varied. Each building must examine their needs through a systematic needs assessment. Once the specific needs are evident, the appropriate prereferral interventions can be implemented.

A group of teachers, support staff, and administrators at the Saw Mill Road Elementary School, North Bellmore, NY (1996) developed an initial referral form in order to provide a mechanism where special and regular educators could consult regarding specific students. (See below).

SAW MILL ROAD ELEMENTARY SCHOOL
EARLY INTERVENTION TEAM
INITIAL REFERRAL FORM
PART 1

This form is to be filled out by the classroom teacher. After completing Part 1 the classroom teacher must meet with a specialist to complete Part 2 of the referral process.

Both parts are to be submitted. NOTE: All EIT forms must be keep in the teacher's class folder, which is located in the office.

Child's Name: _____ Date of Birth: _____

Grade: _____ Teacher's Name: _____ Referral Date: _____

Early Intervention Team Referral Form (Continued)

Please check the items which apply to the child's behaviors or academic performance:

Behaviors

	Disruptive in class		Fidgety, can't stay seated
	Talks out of turn		Disruptive while others are working
	Constantly seeks attention		Overly aggressive to peers
	Fights		Impulsive
	Shy, timid		Quiet
	Does not make friends		Limited Expression of feelings
	Worried, seems anxious		Cries easily, pouts, sulks, seems sad
	Fearful		Does not take risks
	Depends too much on others		Disorganized
	Difficulty following directions		Poor concentration, limited attention span

Academic Performance

Please check the areas in which the child appears to be having difficulties. Where applicable note the child's independent performance level.

	AREA	LEVEL
	Reading	
	Math	
	Writing	
	Concepts	
	Spoken language	
	Articulation difficulties	
	Poor sentence structure	
	Stuttering	
	Written language	
	Spatial organization	

Early Intervention Team Referral Form (*Continued*)

Locomotive Performance

Please check if a child appears to be having difficulties in the following areas:

	Balance
	Coordination
	Eye-hand
	Spatial awareness

SAW MILL ROAD ELEMENTARY SCHOOL
EARLY INTERVENTION TEAM
INITIAL REFERRAL FORM

PART 2

Child's Name: ——————————— Date: ———————————

Teacher's Name: ——————————— Specialist's Name: ———————————

Please describe *the strategies you have tried* in the classroom to help the child:

Strategy   Result

———————————————————————————————

———————————————————————————————

———————————————————————————————

List the *strengths* of the student that might be useful in an intervention:

———————————————————————————————

———————————————————————————————

———————————————————————————————

List sources and summarize findings of background/baseline information, therefore any testing information:

———————————————————————————————

———————————————————————————————

———————————————————————————————

Early Intervention Team Referral Form *(Continued)*

List Special Services the child is currently receiving (if applicable):

_____

_____

_____

Please list the strategies and/or suggestion which were agreed upon by the classroom teacher and specialist after the Part 2 conference:

_____

_____

_____

How will the strategies above be evaluated? Describe the time line which has been determined? (Please specify dates):

_____

_____

_____

Additional information:

Please add any other information you feel is pertinent to the case:

_____

_____

_____

_____

_____

_____

The prereferral strategies developed and implemented by the Seaford Union Free School District have recently been applauded by the commissioner of education of the state of New York. They are listed on the following page:

SEAFORD ELEMENTARY SCHOOLS
PREREFERRAL STRATEGIES

There are numerous interventions or prereferral strategies that are implemented at school prior to a formal CSE referral.

The child study team convenes to discuss/assess a particular student's areas of difficulty and symptoms, and suggest initial strategies:

- Preferential seating in classroom
- Modified assignments or tests
- Extra help after school or during a free period (recess)
- Summer programs to reinforce skills and prevent regression (reading camp)
- Remedial reading
- Remedial math
- Speech/language improvements services
- Short-term counseling
- Referral to outside individual or family counseling (not provided by district)
- Behavior modification
- Placement of student in most appropriate class (i.e., different degrees of structure)
- Multi-age (general education class) vs. traditional
- Different teaching styles
- Placement in class where consultant teacher or other support personnel are available for already classified students
- Written assignment done on computer (word processor)
- Consultation—district occupational therapist works with teachers on informal assessments. Makes recommendations to teachers (in-school activities) and/or parent (home activities) which will correct minor deficits.
- Referral to building team for further consideration of other strategies prior to CSE referral.
- Referral to 504 team (if appropriate)

    Parents are contacted and invited to meetings at every juncture.

SEAFORD MIDDLE/HIGH SCHOOLS
PREREFERRAL STRATEGIES

There are numerous interventions or prereferral strategies that are implemented at school prior to a formal CSE referral.

The student support team convenes to discuss/assess a particular student's areas of difficulty and symptoms, and suggest initial strategies:

- Teacher's input is gleaned at either individual or team meetings. Teaching techniques and approaches are reviewed. Psychologist, special education representative, guidance counselor, social worker, and reading specialist provide insight regarding academics and behavior.

- Parent conferencing is often an early intervention strategy. Informal discussion and obtaining background information/history may be educationally and psychosocially relevant. The psychologist and/or counselor, social worker may conduct this meeting.

- Prudent, applicable classroom management procedures may be given by one of the support staff professionals. Techniques and modifications can be attempted early on, prior to more dramatic steps.

- Implementation of self-help and/or extra tutorial assistance by superior students is provided to assist the student with academic difficulties.

- A reading evaluation may be undertaken when a comprehensive diagnostic battery is recommended by the student support team.

- As a follow up to the above, remedial reading and/or math classes may be implemented to address students' academic deficiencies.

- Clearly, a number of students may be encountering adjustment problems impacting on academic functioning. Issues related to concentration, focus, retrieval, and goal setting need to be addressed in counseling with the psychologist. Parental consent and involvement is pursued. More intensive issues are often referred to outside agencies or mental health professionals requiring long-term treatment. The referring professional maintains routine contact with the outside practitioner.

- Weekly or daily progress reports may provide the student with immediate feedback and encouragement. Additionally, parents are apprised of their child's progress and can more effectively monitor schoolwork.

- Vision and hearing evaluations should be undertaken by the nurse/school doctor if existing symptomology requires such testing.

Seaford Middle/High Schools Prereferral Strategies *(Continued)*

- Appropriate limits and structure may be necessitated by certain behavioral patterns requiring more disciplined response.

- A full medical assessment may be recommended by the SST if it is suspected that a medical condition is contributing to particular problems—i.e., neurologist, ophthalmologist.

- A PINS petition, or "person in need of supervision," entails a family court referral and is made when a student (under the age of 16) is out of control in terms of a combination of behavior, attendance, work pattern, or social maladaptivity.

- A referral to Child Protective Services is indicated if there is a suspicion of neglect. The school is mandated to make such a report if the suspicion is present. A designated SST member, usually counselor psychologist or social worker will file such a report.

Kruger, Sturzziero, Watts, and Vacca (1995) examined the relationship between organized support and satisfaction with teacher assistance teams. Their finding indicated that administrator support was the most important organizational support examined. It far surpassed social support and training. It appears that providing positive feedback to teachers was highly related to Teacher Assistance Team (TAT) satisfaction. The authors suggest the following:

1. Administrators provide staff with positive feedback.

2. Provide a mechanism for team building and social support for members of the TAT.

3. TAT should be self-selected.

4. Provide ongoing evaluation of satisfaction of TAT members and the teachers participating in this collaborative process.

Chalfant and Pysh (1989) describe the teacher assistance teams (TAT) as "a school-based problem-solving unit to assist teachers in generating intervention strategies" (p.50). These teams consist of three elected faculty members. There is variation according to building and administration needs, but at the core of TAT is a forum where teachers can discuss ways to solve building-level problems. These are teacher oriented teams, not intended to supplant special education services. The authors conducted program development studies on ninety-six first-year teachers assistance teams in seven states: Alaska, Arizona, Illinois, Kentucky, Maine, Maryland, and Nebraska.

Their findings are useful for those who are considering such an approach. Three key factors were identified is successful teams; 1) principal support; 2) team attributes, 3) faculty support. Ninety-one percent of the teams note strong support from the building principal as a reason for the effectiveness of the team. Principals provided encouragement for team members, they publicized the team, and supported them through praise and letters of appreciation. Six team attributes were cited as reasons for their effectiveness. They are:

1. Team was well-trained.

2. Team members had a wide range of expertise.

3. TAT has an effective team leader.

4. TAT members were enthusiastic and worked well together.

5. TAT members acted collegially, in a nonthreatening, respectful manner.

6. The team's intervention strategies were successful.

Finally, approximately half of the teams noted the support of their faculty in requesting assistance, attending TAT meetings, implementing intervention, and acting in a prereferral manner as a reason for their effectiveness.

A team approach was employed in a suburban school district that experienced many of the same concerns as large, urban school districts (Lochner and McNamara, 1989). A special education program began to represent a disproportionate percentage of the school population. Consequently, it was perceived as a panacea for any student who was not meeting expectations. Faculty and students alike were isolated from their regular education counterparts. These factors caused an unusually high referral rate to the Committee on Special Education (the team employed for the multidisciplinary team in New York state). For example, during the 1986–1987 school year, there were over fifteen cases per week or over 600 for the year that were referred to the Committee on Special Education for possible special education placement.

An independent audit confirmed that the rate of referral and level of service was higher than expected. Furthermore, because most of these students were not eligible for special education services, the regular education teachers were somewhat frustrated by the perceived lack of action on their referral. The students were still in their classes and they still did not know what to do with them. This is not peculiar to this district. Reports within the professional literature note the price is both costly and ineffective (Algozzine, Christenson, and Ysseldyke, 1982; Graden, Casey and Christenson, 1985). In order to change this two-tiered system of education—one for regular, one for special—a staff-development program was developed and implemented.

Glatthorn (1990) identified seven conditions that were necessary in supporting professional development. They are:

1. There is strong district-level leadership; a district administrator or supervisor coordinates and monitors the entire program.

2. There is a strong leadership at the school level; the principal exercises leadership in fostering norms of collegiality, modeling collaboration, and rewarding teacher cooperation.

3. There is a general climate of openness and trust between administrators and teachers.

4. The cooperative programs are separate from the teacher evaluation process; all data generated in the cooperative programs remain confidential with participants.

5. The cooperative programs have a distinct focus and make use of a shared language.

6. The district provides the resources needed to initiate and sustain the cooperative program.

7. The school makes organizational changes needed to support collaboration; the school schedule enables teachers to work together, staff assignment procedures facilitate cooperation.

This program met these conditions. Initially, the board of education and superintendent of schools made a commitment to provide resources to examine the problem. Building principal's support is another condition necessary for success and this was secured. A superintendent's day conference was scheduled to address the topic of "The Needs of the Atypical Child." Teachers and administrators were included on the planning committee.

Major Components of the Staff Development Program

Consultant Services

A special education consultant, with expertise in the area of learning disabilities was selected to work with the assistant superintendent for administration and pupil personnel services. The role of the consultant was to provide services to staff members in a nonevaluative manner. As noted above, it is critical that this is independent from the teacher evaluation process. The major thrust of the program was to provide technical support and training to all teachers regarding the needs of the atypical learning. Additionally, there was a desire to increase the interaction between regular and special education. This was accomplished through the utilization of building-level teams.

Utilize Building-Level Teams

The use of building-level teams is not a new concept in education. Chalfant and Pysh (1989) note than many school districts throughout the United States utilize school-based support teams. Will (1986) suggest that such teams will enhance the ability of regular educators to service students with learning problems. This concept is not knew to the staff in this district. A "cadre" model has been employed in staff development in the areas of writing, reading, and thinking. This was an important consideration because of the diversity of elementary schools within the community. These unique qualities are reflected in the culture of each school. Building-level teams have allowed for ownership on the part of the building staff and truly reflect specific needs, not global concerns.

Identify Building-Level Team Members

Each building team included at least the following:

> 1 regular education teacher
>
> 1 special education teacher
>
> 1 speech language pathologist
>
> 1 school psychologist

Membership on the team was voluntary and only those staff members who were positively disposed to the project were included. And although these (n=40) were highly motivated staff members, an incentive program was also implemented. Each member received two in-service credits for the first year of the project and one credit per year for each subsequent year. These credits can be applied toward their salary increments. They also were allowed to attend workshops (substitute coverage for their class was provided) and received consultant support. The major responsibilities of the cadre were:

1. To provide technical support and training to all teachers in their building in relation to working with atypical children.

2. To make several presentations to their faculty.

3. To followup with staff and administrators regarding problems, solutions, or additional needs.

In order to proceed with these responsibilities, a needs assessment had to be developed.

Building-Level Needs Assessment

Each building-level team identified the needs of their colleagues. A consensus of 75 percent was reached, and the list of needs was prioritized. It was important to have each team responsible for its own needs assessment. In this way it was not imposed on them from central administration, and they were able to identify the concerns of their colleagues based on their day-to-day interaction.

Program Implementation

Initial Training. Each team was responsible for developing and implementing a "presentation" to their colleagues based upon the results of the needs assessment. Prior to the presentation the entire group (n=40) met with the consultant and the assistant superintendent for administration and pupil personnel services for a training session. They were provided with a wide variety of formats and had an opportunity to plan and be provided with feedback from the other building teams. For many, this was the first time they even made a presentation to their colleagues. Therefore, considerable effort went into allaying their anxiety, providing ample preparation time, and reinforcing their efforts.

The formats employed were as varied as the topics (see below). The entire faculty evaluated each session. The feedback was utilized in the development of the ongoing program throughout the school year.

A SAMPLE OF FORMATS AND TOPICS EMPLOYED IN IN-SERVICE PROGRAMS

FORMAT

- lecture
- video tape
- simulations
- small group process
- large group activities
- films
- audio tapes

A Sample of Formats and Topics Employed in In-Service Programs (*Continued*)

PRESENTATIONS

- identification of special needs
- characteristics of atypical learners
- attention deficit disorder
- behavior management
- what's so special about special education?
- modifying instructions
- remediating language disorders

Ongoing Training.   Throughout the school year building-level teams met to provide training for their colleagues. Two group meetings addressed the needs of the team in their buildings.

A booklet was developed by the entire group, the consultant, and the assistant superintendent in order to have a tangible product to give all the district staff members. The contents of the booklet were as follows:

1. Special Education Categories

2. Effective Teaching Methods (Academic)

3. Effective Teaching Methods (Behavioral)

As each team develops yearly goals, the members continue to receive support and training via consultative services and group training sessions. And while the needs of each building continued to vary, they can all be subsumed under the major goal of the project—to provide all teachers with the skills necessary to teach atypical learners.

Impact

Anecdotal reports suggest the staff development program described herein was successful. Administrators and teachers appeared to be very positive about the functioning of the teams. It is not often a "one-shot deal." Regular and special educators were provided with opportunities for inter-action. They realized that they can solve many of their problems through collaborative efforts. There have also been more quantifiable results of this partnership:

- The rate of referral to the committee on special education has dropped from fifteen per week (over 600 per year) in 1986–1987 to six per week (240 per year) in 1989–1990.

- The enrollment in special education programs has dropped from 1125 in 1986 to 901 in 1989.

- Only one member asked to be removed from a team.

- An increasing number of staff members have asked to become members of the building-level team.

Summary

The needs of all students can be addressed if the needs of all teachers are addressed. A well-developed program aimed at providing teachers with the skills necessary to teach all children has yielded tangible and intangible results. Through the utilization of school-based teams a new partnership between regular and special educators has emerged.

The employment of such building-level teams has found support in the professional literature and advocacy groups. Among the many recommendations suggested in *Segregated and Second Rate: Special Education in New York* (Advocates for Children, 1992) are the following related to collaborative, problem-solving teams:

- Create support and informational networks for teachers to share strategies for and experiences in educating disabled children in the regular classroom.

- Develop consultant-teacher and team-teaching strategies and adopt conclusive models.

- Establish a new continuum of intermediate, preventive services, which provide students with individualized support prior to special education referral.

Collaboration is not a simple process as the case study provided by Reeve and Hallahan (1994) illustrates:

Yours, Mine, or Ours?

As a resource teacher for eighth-grade students with learning disabilities or behavior disorders, Steve Franklin believed his first priority was to ensure his students' success in their mainstream classes. Thus, when he heard about the inclusion model—in the form of the resource teacher working in the regular education class with his students and others; actual team-teaching potential—Steve was excited. He was only a first-year teacher at Wilson Junior High, however, and he did not want to "step on any toes."

He had heard that the English teacher with whom his students would be placed was excellent with special needs students—demanding, expecting the best, but not unrealistic in her expectations. These qualities, Steve thought, would help ease him, as well as his students, into this new inclusion model. Here, perhaps, would be a place where not only the children would feel part of the mainstream, but Steve as well could feel the satisfaction of working with students on a huge continuum of strengths, abilities, and weaknesses in the general classroom.

Two weeks remained in the summer before the start of the school year, and Steve wasted no time in starting to build rapport with this teacher. He called her one evening to set up a meeting.

"Hello, Pam, this is Steve Franklin. I've just been hired as the resource teacher next year, and I understand you'll be teaching most of my students English. Would it be possible for us to get together sometime soon to discuss possibilities for how we envision our working roles and get to know each other's styles?"

"Sure. Let's meet at my house next Tuesday. Right after noon is good for me. My kids are napping!"

"Great. I'll see you then. I'm really looking forward to this. I've heard great things about your work with special needs students in your classroom."

On the appointed day, Steve and Pam had a productive discussion about the inclusion model. Pam was highly receptive to the proposal, saying that in her twenty years of teaching, several special educators had worked with her in this capacity and that most often it was successful. She stressed that person styles and philosophies played a key role in these interactions. If the teachers kept open communication, she found, the students invariable benefited from this combination of professionals working toward similar goals for them.

That first day of school, in seventh-period English in room 317, two teachers stood in front of the room. They introduced themselves to the students as Mr. Franklin and Ms. Jarinski, not differentiating their respective roles as special educator and general educator. For some of the resource students, even, this was their first contact with Mr. Franklin.

Steve and Pam stayed after school late that day to plan the first semester's goals and assignments further, after having the advantage of meeting the students with whom they'd be dealing. Steve was fascinated by Pam's creativity. He also was pleased to hear that Pam's expectations were no lower for his students than for the others, although she was amenable to his suggestions for certain accommodations. For example, Pam wanted students to read *The Outsiders* and write a summary and reactions to each chapter. Knowing that reading this book, let alone writing detailed analyses, would be difficult for some of his students, Steve created audiotapes for each chapter of the students with particularly low reading ability. Also for those who could read fairly well (i.e., at grade level) but who shied away from written language assignments, he thought that taking dictation of their summaries and reactions would be a more effective first novel-of-the-year measure of their comprehension. Pam seemed to be pleased with these accommodations, so Steve felt reassured that she would be open to others he might make in the upcoming year.

Each day Steve looked forward to seventh period. This was a time when he could work with a range of students' ability levels that he hoped would afford a "reality check," a measure against which he could gauge the performance of the students in his caseload. Also, he could see in the regular classroom what behavior and learning differences differentiated his students from the others. For example, Chris took an extra several minutes to get his materials out; Sherika talked constantly, it seemed, to her neighbor (whomever it may be that day); Shawn and Joe couldn't keep their hands to themselves; April gazed out of the window when directions were given; and Charles, being teased a lot for his weight and "strange" behaviors (picking his nose, talking to himself), always seemed dejected.

Because of all of these individual differences and occasional need for crisis intervention, Steve's role in the classroom began to evolve from what he had originally planned. Suddenly, it seemed, Pam was the teacher in the front of the blackboard while Steve "floated" through the classroom arena, helping to clarify directions, organizing students, editing students' writing, administering positive reinforcement to students who were behaving appropriately and on task, and defusing fights before they could erupt (or dealing with the postaltercation discipline).

Frustrated and unsure of the situation, he asked Pam, "Am I doing a good job? I don't intend to sound unrealistic, but is this the way it's worked with the resource teachers involved in inclusion in the past?"

"Steve, you're doing a fabulous job; I don't think I could reach this group if I didn't have your help. The things you do in class are so valuable for all of the kids, not just the identified students."

"Yeah, but I often think that if you didn't have to deal with the tough emotional and learning needs of my kids, your day would go much smoother. I wish I could do more for your than I do."

"Hey, Steve, they're not just your kids—they're ours."

This woman was like a special educator's dream: her concepts of inclusion and her philosophy about the special needs children were so great they were almost a cliché! Always in the back of Steve's mind, however, was the knowledge that this team of teachers, led by Pam Jarinski, did not have to take Steve's caseload every year. Pam and Steve did not make any more money than the rest of the teachers in the school, yet they dealt with some tough issues with the students with specific disabilities. Steve wanted to know that he and his students would be invited back to this classroom next year and for years to come.

Difficulties in the seventh-period class continued. Steve and Pam anticipated this class less and less as the year went on. By the second nine-week grading period, Steve notices that not just "his students" were difficult to instruct in this setting. Of course, part of the problem was that this was the last period of the day, and interactions had built to the boiling point with some of the eighth graders by the time they got to the Franklin/Jarinski connection. Also, energy levels were low for students who weren't out of their seat or talking with others. Some seemed as if they could use that afternoon nap afforded to the lucky kindergartners! Looking at the "tired" ones made Pam and Steve feel even less successful. The ultimate frustration for them, however, was the disappointed, rolling-of-eyes look on the faces of the students who were there each day ready to learn but who had to wait out the disruptions of the students around them.

Steve continued to do much of the "behind the scenes" work, planning and organizing differentiated activities of the class, but he worked less and less in front of the class. Although Pam and Steve never spoke of it, it became evident that this was the way they would work the class, but he worked less and less in front of the class. Although Pam and Steven never spoke of it, it became evident that this was the way they would work the class: Pam in front, giving instruction, and Steve still "floating." He thought back to their original meeting and the emphasis Pam had put on communication. They both were so busy keeping up with the kids, however, that they barely had time to talk except when they saw each other in seventh period. Once there, they were two people in the same room doing entirely different jobs! While Pam had her planning period, Steve was pulling kids from their Enriching Arts classes, so he had a full resource class of six students. Occasionally he could scoot next door to set plans for the day, but the two teachers rarely had the opportunity to sit down and discuss the many and varied interactions, responses, and difficulties that transpired each day during seventh period.

Steve was beginning to have serious difficulties with the concept of teacher collaborative as it was manifesting itself in room 317. Although he maintained the utmost professional and person respect for Pam, he could not help believing that this situation was not best serving his students or feeling dissatisfied with the team-teaching responsibilities he had hoped for.

Steve's internal pressure to do better got worse one day when a critique came from a new, unexpected source: a student. Shawn, one of the students with behavior disorder, had continued to have trouble keeping his hands to himself, despite the contracts and self-monitoring strategies Steve had worked on with him. One day Steve had approached Shawn's desk, knelt down, and whispered to him to give Lucy's pencil back to her. Shawn turned away from him, saying, "You're not the teacher here anyway. You're the resource teacher. You should be in your room helping kids and stuff."

Steve's first thought was, "Who is this little guy to tell me how I should do my job?" His second thought was to realize that only he, but other kids as well, were confused about Steve's role. Their experiences with their resource teachers most likely would have been with the pull-out model. Also, they did not know all of the behind-the-scenes planning Steve did with Pam. What they saw each day in the class did not look much like a teacher partnership.

One day the behavior of the class was particularly horrendous, bad enough that both Pam and Steve decided to spend some heartfelt, dedicated time after the long day to discuss their next move. The idea they came up with for behavior management was to group the students into teams and give each team token reinforcement for appropriate behaviors (e.g., attention-to-task, helping teammates, having materials out) and removing it for inappropriate behaviors (e.g., talking out, not having materials, not attending to task). The teachers were clear about the parameters for this system when they presented it to the students, and they believed it was not too complicated to work.

The physical change within the classroom was fairly radical: Steve and Pam moved all of the desks to an empty room at the end of the hall and exchanged them for tables. They arranged the student into groups of four, mixing ability levels but minimizing interaction and behavior difficulties. The tokens they gave were "fake" money bills that each group could amass and cash in at the end of the grading period. Each group's name was on the board, and money was taken away or given as deserved in the appropriate column so the students would see their accumulation and loss of rewards immediately.

This plan was fairly successful for a few weeks. The students motivated the others in their group to work hard, stay on task, and behave appropriately. When student "messed up," Pam or Steve was not always the person calling them on it. Now the students had a major role in behavior management.

Steve, however, still had a minimal part in the plan, as far as classroom time was concerned. Pam was the one in front of the room with the chalk, so by mere fact of physical proximity to the "rewards" board, she was one to award and withdraw tokens. Steve had hoped this system would have afforded him a higher profile in the class.

After the novelty had worn off the token system, problems continued in the classroom. Pam and Steve realized that keeping up with the system demanded more of their time and patience than they had hoped. Steve was disappointed that this was not working, but it was helpful for him to see that strategies that might work in a smaller group or self-contained special education setting were far more difficult to implement with the large group. As always, his admiration for Pam's job did not change.

Steve was late to seventh period the next Monday, as he'd gotten his finger caught in his file cabinet rushing to tie up loose ends from sixth period, and he went to the clinic to put ice on it. It's amazing what can happen when you're gone for ten minutes.

He came to room 317, opened the door, and way many somber faces in front of him. They all looked at him and then as Ms. Jarinski. Steve sat down next to her at the table and furrowed his brow for some explanation about what was going on. Pam handed him a list of four names, all resource students, and said, loud enough for all students to hear, "I think we have to self-contain these kids for the rest of the year. It goes against my philosophy, but they just can't seem to control themselves."

Yes, only three weeks remained in school, but Steve was shocked. Without changing their IEPs, this would not be legal, and he believed this should not be the final solution, nor was it the message he wanted to send these kids: that they are incapable of controlling their behavior and, thus, cannot be accepted in the mainstream English class. What could he do without damaging his relationship with Pam? (pp. 402–7)

They suggest that educators examine the process carefully and address the following questions:

- What focus can collaboration take in the classroom?

- What competencies do special and general education teachers need?

- What are the major barriers?

- What are the potential benefits?

Issues and Concerns

Prereferral interventions have been on the increase. In fact, thirty-four states require or recommend them (Carter and Sugai, 1989). However, the professional literature suggests that there are barriers to overcome. Johnson, Pugach, and Hammittee (1988) wonder why consultation has not been widely implemented. They cite the following barriers:

1. The definition of "consultant"

2. Insufficient time and overwhelming caseloads

3. Credibility of special educators

4. The match between the thinking of general and special education

5. Hierarchical relationships

6. Knowledge base

1. *Definition.* The role of the consultant is rarely clearly defined and there is confusion as to who can fill this role. The problem is that if the special educator is always the consultant, the implication is they have skills not held by the regular educator.

2. *Insufficient time and overwhelming caseloads.* This is clearly a problem in urban centers where the class size is higher than their suburban counterpart. Teachers simply don't have the time to meet.

3. *Credibility of special educators.* It is not unusual for regular educators to think the special educators have an easy job. This, coupled with the lack of experience in regular classrooms, may lead to problems of credibility.

4. *The match between the thinking of general and special educators.* Too often the strategies suggested by special educators may not appear to be appropriate or easily implemented in the regular classroom. This may be due to different experiences or training.

5. *Hierarchical relationship.* As long as special educators are perceived as "experts," rather than a professional who is on an equal level with regular educators, the process is doomed to failure.

6. *Knowledge bases.* Finally, the competencies of special and regular educators are different. This needs to be bridged by teacher training institutions if all parties are to communicate effectively.

Pugach and Johnson (1988) expand on their concerns and suggest ways to overcome these limitations:

1. Consultation should be a reciprocal, mutual activity among all professionals in a school.

2. Consultation should facilitate independent problem solving on the part of several educators.

3. Consultation should be a routine part of interpersonal interaction and daily functioning.

4. The language used to discuss consultation should reflect its centrality to the school as a whole and not only its relationship to special education.

They also note that the term pre, as in prereferral, is that we are doing something while we wait for special education or that we only employ such strategies when we are considering special education service. This leads to a reactive rather than a proactive approach.

Pugach and Lawrence (1989) believe that if this process is to work, it must be thought of in the broader context of educational reform, not merely under the domain of special education. They posit assumptions that address this concern:

1. Prereferral is a function of special education

2. Consultation is a multidirectional activity

3. Classroom teachers have adequate expertise to solve many classroom problems in the absence of specialists, given time and appropriate structure to do so.

4. All problems do not require the same configuration of educators to develop solutions.

For culturally and linguistically diverse students, the assumptions would reinforce problem solving solutions and eliminate the current practice where these students are referred for special education services at a disproportionate rate.

Finally, based on several years of research, Fuchs and Fuchs (1994) identified a number of salient features of prereferral intervention. They are:

1. School systems interested in implementing prereferral intervention must build such activity into the job descriptions of support staff selected as consultants. School psychologists typically will not be capable of fulfilling such a role on top of a busy schedule of testing. Likewise, resource room teachers cannot be expected to provide direct service to a full caseload of students and also function as consultants.

2. A consultant or team of consultants should be responsible for the overall direction of the prereferral effort.

3. Consultants must receive adequate training (a) in the process of consultation, (b) in understanding completely the classroom intervention(s) to be used, and (c) in how to implement such interventions so as to cause the least disruption and burden to the teacher and classmates of the targeted pupil.

4. The consultation process must be efficient. Because school time is precious, the process must be careful structured to include only activity that is essential to achieve desired outcomes, and the participants should always be time-conscious.

5. As to the previous point, however, consultants cannot cut corners with the process. That is, lack of time may not be used as an excuse to eliminate essential aspects of consultation such as (a) defining problem behavior; (b) setting explicit goals for students or teachers; (c) collecting reliable and valid data on performance observed before, during, and after implementation of the intervention; and (d) conducting systematic formative evaluation or intervention effectiveness.

6. The classroom interventions must be acceptable to teacher, which, first and foremost, means they should be feasible. This very important characteristic cannot be defined in the absolute, because what is feasible to one teacher, may not be feasible to another. Thus, the consultant must define and redefine feasibility with each and every teacher.

7. There must be provision for ensuring the fidelity of the classroom interventions. In other words, consultants must be certain that teachers and students implementing the interventions do so according to the manner in which they were instructed.

8. As indicated, data on student or teacher behavior should be collected at multiple points during the consultation process, and these data should be socially valid. One means of accomplishing this is to obtain consumer satisfaction information. Teachers, students, and consultants should be encouraged to express their comprehension, thoughts, feelings, and overall

evaluation of the process. They should also be asked to make recommendations for improving the effort.

Special educators in urban settings must develop an understanding of the diverse population in the school and community. The evaluation checklist provided by Davidman and Davidman (1994) can clearly be translated into skills, knowledge, and attitudes that all special educators should demonstrate:

EVALUATION CHECKLIST

____1. The special educator values and respects cultural diversity in all forms and degrees.

____2. The special educator recognizes differences between handicapping conditions and cultural diversity rather than perceiving differences as liabilities or deficiencies in need of remediation.

____3. The special educator coordinates the efforts of administrators, faculty, and staff in the provision of the least restrictive environment for culturally diverse handicapped learners.

____4. The special educator supports a racially and culturally diverse faculty and staff for all handicapped youngsters.

____5. The special educator insists that screening and placement procedures recognize cultural diversity and that such procedures follow the legal mandates and guidelines for providing special education experiences.

____6. The special educator works with parents and families on a regular basis, helps them understand programs for the handicapped, and make referrals to appropriate social service agencies.

____7. The special educator provides screening with testing and assessment instruments with the least racial, cultural, and social class bias.

____8. The special educator provides screening with testing and assessment instruments with the least racial, cultural, and social class bias.

____9. The special educator plans learning experiences that recognize differences in language and dialectical backgrounds.

____10. The special educator supports community recognition and efforts to provide appropriate educational experiences for culturally diverse handicapped learners.

3

Assessment Practices

Assessment models used to evaluate underachieving students in urban areas typically consist of a fixed battery of standardized and informal assessment instruments or a battery of varied instruments, which may differ from student to student at the discretion of the assessor. A basic premise of this text is that no single battery of standardized or informal assessment instruments should be expected to completely describe the full range of any student's achievement or potential.

When attempting to document the performance of students who represent diverse linguistic and cultural experiences, it is especially important that the educational assessment model be student-specific and derived from and guided by a set of carefully constructed diagnostic questions. If, as is often the case, the assessment model permits individual assessment instruments to drive the educational assessment, then the assessment instruments themselves very often become the framework for the educational questions, answers, and interventions. For example, if an informal or standardized measure of auditory perception is the routine initial assessment to be administered to all referred students, a student who appears to be underachieving in reading and achieves a score that is below the average range on this instrument, may easily be viewed as having a deficit in auditory perception. The presumed deficit in auditory perception is then viewed as the cause of the suspected reading problem. The student may then be "diagnosed" as having a reading disability resulting from a deficit in auditory perception. Educational intervention might then consist of training in auditory perception until the student achieves a score on the auditory perception assessment instrument within the average range.

In fact, the presenting problem may not be related to auditory perceptual deficits. The student's below average score on the assessment of auditory

45

perception may not represent a true deficit in information processing, and the remediation of the conjectured deficit in auditory perception may not result in actual improvement in the original presenting problem, underachievement in reading.

If we wish to measure a student's ability to perform such tasks as repeating digits backwards, reading single words aloud, and distinguishing minimal pairs, the evaluator must understand the theoretical basis from which such tasks rise and the relationship of these activities to the desired academic performance and to the original reason for referral. The selection and administration of assessment instruments must, therefore, follow the logic of carefully constructed diagnostic questions, which guide the assessment. That is, a logical, coherent set of questions that address the perceived academic problem must become the guiding force of the assessment instead of individual assessment instruments. It is often argued that testing should not drive instruction. More importantly, tests should not drive assessment. Rather, tests and testlike procedures, in conjunction with other information regarding student achievement, can inform the assessment process.

Furthermore, that any hypothesis regarding student achievement or ability, which is generated from an educational assessment, must be grounded on multiple forms of evidence regarding student performance (Chittenden, 1991). Standardized test results, performance data, and observational data from teachers, parents, and other informants must be collected, and thoughtful decisions will have to be made to allow for systematic collection of evidence over time and in a variety of settings. It should also be noted that even the most comprehensive assessment may not result in irrefutable evidence of specific learning disabilities. In such cases, continued observation, data collection, and carefully monitored instructional modifications can be conducted. The following principles can guide a thoughtful assessment of student performance, which considers issues of cultural and linguistic diversity.

Guiding Principles for a Model of Educational Assessment

It is proposed that educational assessment be led by the following principles:

1. There must be a clear definition of the purpose of the assessment.

2. Diagnostic questions must guide the assessment.

3. Multiple forms of evidence of student performance must be gathered.

4. Evidence of achievement must be gathered over time and in a variety of contexts.

5. Evidence of student performance must be based on curriculum materials and experiences that are familiar to the student.

6. Evaluators must be able to accept lack of closure.

Clear Definition of the Purpose of the Assessment

A thorough educational assessment should not begin with administration of a routine standardized test, but rather with a clear delineation of the purpose of the assessment and its expected outcomes. The issues to be addressed in this initial phase include:

a. A description of the presenting problem by the person making the referral, and

b. Specific diagnostic questions, and

c. An outline of the assessment outcomes expected by the person making the referral and by others involved with the student.

Often the person making the referral may simply need to discuss the perceived academic problem with another person who has knowledge of the student's behavior. This may be an educational evaluator, a parent, or another of the students' teachers. A focused discussion of what is perceived to be atypical learning or behavior can result in a better understanding of the student's achievement and in the attempt to modify instruction within the classroom. Smith, Dowdy, Polloway, and Blalock (1997) have developed a form that is helpful in documenting such interventions (see below):

The following prereferral intervention strategies will be implemented for _____ beginning _____. The results of these strategies will be reviewed on _____ by the child study team.

	No. of days attempted	Problem better	No change	Problem worse
Teaching Strategies				
Taped or oral presentation/testing	___	___	___	___
Modeling	___	___	___	___
Preteach vocabulary	___	___	___	___
Slower pace	___	___	___	___

	No. of days attempted	Problem better	No change	Problem worse
Teaching Strategies *(continued)*				
Alternative/additional materials	___	___	___	___
Tutoring-peers, volunteers, paraprofessionals	___	___	___	___
Guided practice	___	___	___	___
Special grouping	___	___	___	___
Task Requirements				
Change criteria for success	___	___	___	___
Break into smaller steps	___	___	___	___
Provide prompts	___	___	___	___
Clarify directions	___	___	___	___
Behavior Techniques				
Behavior management (attach explanation)	___	___	___	___
Student contract	___	___	___	___
Consultation with	___	___	___	___
Sessions with school counselor	___	___	___	___
Other (describe)	___	___	___	___
_____	___	___	___	___
_____	___	___	___	___
_____	___	___	___	___
_____	___	___	___	___

Team members present: _____

_____

In addition, a clear understanding of the anticipated outcomes of an educational assessment is crucial. Is the assessment being conducted for the purpose of classification, for design of instructional procedures, or a change in placement? These issues need to be explicitly stated and made clear to all concerned so that the diagnostic questions may be appropriately framed.

Diagnostic Questions Must Guide the Assessment

A model is proposed in which diagnostic questions are the underpinnings of the educational assessment. Messick (1987) has proposed that assessment be conducted within three contexts:

a. the interpersonal student context;

b. the sociocultural context in which the student functions or has functioned; and

c. the instructional context of the school.

Sets of diagnostic questions must be designed to explore each context. Typically, a battery of tests is administered to investigate only the intrapersonal student context and to answer the question, *What's wrong with this student?* However, it is particularly important in the assessment of culturally and linguistically diverse students that the sociocultural and instructional contexts be as carefully scrutinized as the individual student. Questions should be designed to formulate hypotheses regarding: 1) the probability of the actual existence of the presenting problem; and, if it does appear to exist, 2) the contribution of cultural, linguistic, socioeconomic, instructional, psychological, and physical factors to the problem.

Diagnostic Questions Regarding Student Context

In the assessment of specific learning disabilities, one critical question is being posed: Is there sufficient information, from multiple forms of evidence, to conclude that perceived underachievement is the result of a pathological condition inherent to the student that warrants a special education classification and placement?

Diagnostic Questions Regarding Sociocultural Context

Do cultural factors interfere with the student's ability to master the content, as presented?

Do cultural factors interfere with the referring person's ability to observe the full range of the student's ability and achievement?

Do linguistic factors preclude the student from benefiting from the current instructional approach?

Do linguistic factors preclude the student from demonstrating his or her ability and content mastery?

Do socioeconomic factors interfere with the student's ability to master and demonstrate the content in the current instructional setting?

Diagnostic Questions Regarding Instructional Context

Underachievement is a hallmark of specific learning disabilities. However, it is often difficult to determine if the underachievement of many urban students is a reflection of lack of adequate instruction or a student-specific information processing problem. Messick (1987) suggests four general areas of instructional context questioning for special education referrals:

1. "Evidence that the school is using programs and curricula shown to be effective not just for students in general but for the various ethnic, linguistic, and socioeconomic groups actually served by the school in question."

2. "Evidence that the teacher has implemented the curriculum effectively for the student in question—for example, that the student received appropriate direction, feedback, and reinforcement, that the student has been adequately exposed to the curriculum by virtue of not having missed many lessons due to absence or disciplinary exclusions from class, and so forth."

3. "Evidence that the student has not learned what was taught while, at the same time, other students in the class are performing acceptably."

4. "There should be documentation that systematic efforts were made to identify learning difficulties and strengths and to take corrective action or employ alternative instructional methods and materials." (pp. 9–10)

Multiple Forms of Evidence of Student Performance Must be Gathered

Student-specific diagnostic questions should drive the assessment and a variety of forms of evidence regarding student ability and achievement. These questions can then be answered. The conclusions regarding general ability and mastery of content should not be based on performance in a single instance on a single assessment format. Nor should such conclusions be based on the observations of a single informant.

Leung (1996) suggests that those responsible for the assessment of culturally and linguistically diverse students employ six "quality" indicators:

- Examination of opportunity to learn

- Involvement of parents or caretakers

- Use only trained interpreters

- Nonreliance on psychometrics
- Full use of a multidisciplinary team
- Use of informal clinical judgment

He encouraged evaluators to examine multiple evidence or they will likely miss a significant part of what a child knows. He cautions against data collection procedures that go according to plan. We need to be suspicious of an evaluation that is ordinary with a population that is extraordinary.

Multiple forms of evidence in a variety of contexts, consisting of traditional standardized tests, performance assessments and portfolios, parent/teacher observations and interviews are necessary (Chittenden, 1991). The use of traditional standardized tests should be minimal, in particular because of the ongoing criticism of such instruments. Poteet, Choate, and Stewart (1996) summarize the problems with traditional assessment. They are:

1. *Misleading information.* The results from traditional tests provide a limited view of student learning. Choate and Evans (1992) noted that many classroom skills are not assessed by traditional tests because the tests sample a broad range of skills. Test results can mislead the consumer because many people think the score is an absolute rather than merely an indicator. Furthermore, test scores do not explain the approach students take when responding to test items. Some students who can perform a given test item successfully fail the item for reasons not related to their knowledge of the correct answer (e.g., test anxiety, feeling sick or sleepy, effects of medications, or difficulty marking answer sheets). Thus, using these tests to make decisions about students' futures (e.g., if they will pass reading) may result in incorrect decisions. A "good" (valid) test has good (accurate) predictive validity; many standardized norm-referenced tests do not.

2. *Unfairness.* Many of the traditional tests are unfair to certain populations in America, particularly some students with disabilities (Choate, Enright, Miller, Poteet, and Rakes, 1992). They are biased in the sense that the language usage, cultural examples, and learning styles or skills required to successfully complete test items do not reflect those of populations such as people with limited English proficiency, low incomes, and membership in certain minority or cultural groups and females. Some tests tend to favor middle to upper-class white males (Neil and Medina, 1989).

3. *Distraction.* Test results often are used as measures of accountability—for example, in reaching reading objectives and goals and as yardsticks for comparing schools to determine which is "better" (has higher average scores). When these factors are emphasized, attention is distracted from

social issues that may contribute to low average scores-overcrowded class-rooms, lack of adequate instructional materials, administrative focus on test scores rather than on acquiring knowledge, high-level thinking, and so on.

4. *Quality control.* Testing is a big business in America. The taxpayer cost of state and local testing is approaching $1 billion a year. Students at some grade levels are taking as many as twelve comprehensive tests in a single year (Moses, 1990.) However, there is no authority to guarantee regulations or quality control, although recent demands for alternative assessment may eventually result in quality control.

5. *Expense.* Traditional testing is quite expensive in terms of cost of materials and time (administering, scoring, posting results). The money allocated for traditional testing in a school budget might best be allocated to other approaches to assessment that are less expensive, more time-efficient, less biased, and produce results that have more meaning for educational decisions.

6. *Use of results.* Standardized tests all too often are used unfairly to shut Americans out of education and employment opportunities (Moses, 1990). In an interview with Kirst (1991), Lorrie Shepard pointed out that when tests drive instruction, the curriculum often covers only what is on the test. Teaching to the test—at least when the test is a standardized multiple-choice test—restricts the curriculum to covering test items that are rather factual, concrete, and isolated from a broader integrated scope of desired curricula. Hanson (1993) portrayed tests as the gatekeepers, allowing only some individuals to pass through. He suggested that test scores can redefine an individual in the eyes of the individual and in the eyes of others.

7. *Sending the wrong message to students.* Traditional tells foster a one-right-answer mentality, limiting students' thinking processes. Although some knowledge actually has only one correct answer, other knowledge (e.g., causes of the Civil War), has no one right answer (Hambleton and Maurphy, 1991) (pp. 213–14). The following are some guidelines for the types of forms of evidence that may lead to a better understanding of the academic performance of ethnically and linguistically diverse urban students.

Grossman (1996) cited additional criticism of standardized assessment as they apply to students for culturally and linguistically diverse backgrounds:

- Standardized assessment procedures do not accurately or validly describe how students function in the present nor do they predict how students will function in the future.

- They ask "Do you know what I know?" rather than "What is it that you know?"

- The data collected with standardized instruments are typically collected in nonclassroom situations under unusual circumstances by unfamiliar assessors, and therefore do not reflect how students function in real life classrooms with real life teachers.

- Percentile ranking, grade-level placements, and other norms provided by standardized tests are not realistic because national norms are not necessarily true for a given school district, school district, school, or class. The content of courses taught at the seventh-grade level in a predominantly middle-class suburban school may be very different than the course content in a school serving predominantly poor urban students. Thus, students who score at the seventh-grade level on a nationally normed reading test may actually be functioning much lower than the typical seventh-grade student in a middle-class neighborhood suburban school and much higher than the typical seventh-grade student in some other school districts.

- Standardized assessment procedures are not easily adapted to students' contextual, cultural, and linguistic characteristics.

- They measure different attributes with different groups of students. When used with limited-English-proficient, non-European American and poor students, they measure what students have been exposed to, how fast they can work without making careless mistakes, how motivated they are to succeed and do their best, how well they can adapt to the particular format of the procedure, how they respond to pressure, and so on, not their achievement, learning potential, learning disabilities, or whatever else they may measure learning potential, learning disabilities, or whatever else they may measure when used with European American middle-class students who are English proficient and speak standard English.

- They require all students to fit a preconceived mold. "Despite the lip service we pay to the myriad ways in which individuals differ, and claim to celebrate this variety, our practices speak otherwise. In fact it is performance on these tests—with their narrow and rigid definition both of when children should be able to perform particular skills and how they should be able to exhibit their knowledge—that determines whether we see children as okay or not. In the process we damage all children—we devalue the variety of strength they bring them to school. All differences become handicaps."

This is not meant to propose the total elimination of all standardized assessments from educational assessments. Indeed, when it is important to assess mastery of very specific information, the most efficient and economical assessment instrument may be an appropriate standardized test.

The Council of America Psychological Association (as cited in Grossman [1996]) stated:

> Good psychological decisions require good evidence, and some of the most useful and reliable evidence comes from well-designed and properly interpreted standardized tests . . . Yet for a variety of reasons, some valid and some not, testing has been the constant target of attack, joined in often by political figures or by the popular media. Testing continues to play an informative role in psychological decisions, for example in counseling practice and educational guidance, yet the science and profession of psychology are damaged by lopsided attacks, which often go without correction, comment or rebuttal.
>
> Now, therefore, the Council of the American Psychological Association asserts the following:
>
> 1. Standardized testing, competently administered and evaluated, is a valuable tool in individual, educational, and personnel decision-making.
>
> 2. Abuses of testing, through unwarranted labeling or interpretation, are to be avoided as are abuses of any valuable tool." (p. 283)

The problem is that the traditional standardized test instruments that have been used in the assessment of learning disabilities often have shortcomings in urban settings. Some questions raised by the use of traditional norm-referenced standardized tests with diverse populations include:

Does the test or a subtest of an instrument answer the diagnostic questions generated by the assessment team?

Are the specific student's educational and cultural experiences represented by the normative population?

How are the results of the student's performance on the standardized test going to be used?

What inferences regarding the student's ability and achievement will be made from the score obtained on the standardized instrument?

Performance Assessments and Portfolios

In response to a growing dissatisfaction with traditional standardized multiple-choice item formats, a national interest in "performance"-based assessments is developing. These alternative assessments consist of such activities as open-ended responses, portfolios, and performances. In general, these instruments are highly contextualized so that items are imbedded in a context that is within the student's range of reallife experiences. Some researches have used the term "authentic" assessments. Pike and Salend (1995) compare traditional assessment to authentic assessment procedures.

Traditional Assessment. Traditionally, educational decisions are based on assessment data collected through the use of teacher administered norm referenced, standardized tests (Salend, 1994). Norm-referenced testing offers educators information that allows comparisons of the student's performance to norms that are based on the scores of others. While norm-referenced testing is often employed to determine eligibility for special education services, it fails to provide specific information for planning, implementing, and evaluating a student's educational program. Norm-referenced test scores tend to be static and reflect only one score on a particular day under certain conditions. They do not reveal a student's attempts toward determining correct answers, nor do they acknowledge the student's efforts.

Authentic Assessment. Authentic assessment refers to a variety of informal and formal student-centered strategies for collecting and recording information about students. Authentic assessment practices seek to facilitate student learning by linking assessment and instruction. Authentic assessment procedures emphasize both the process and products of learning, and place value on input from teachers and students (Anthony, Johnson, Mickelson, and Preece, 1991). Teachers who effectively use authentic assessment practices continuously observe and interact with their students to discover not only what students know, but also how students learn. For authentic assessment to be meaningful for students and teachers, it should encompass the following principles:

- Assessment should be linked to what students are actually learning and what they might be learning.

- Assessment should be viewed as a continuous and cumulative process.

- Assessment should be conducted throughout the school day and across the curriculum.

- Assessment results should be based on data from a variety of assessment strategies.

- Assessment should occur during real learning experiences.

- Assessment should be a collaborative process on the part of students and teachers.

- Assessment findings should be easily communicated to students, parents, professionals, administrators, and other decision makers. (Department of Education, Wellington, 1989; Pike, Compain, and Mumper, 1994)

Effective authentic assessment strategies involve students in the assessment process and make them the focus of all evaluation activities. Research indicates that student academic achievement levels and study behaviors are enhanced when students are involved in establishing the standards for performance (Brownell, Colleti, Ersner-Hershfled, Hershfeld, and Wilson, 1977). Salend (1983) found that students' performance levels as measured via self-assessment procedures were superior to the performance levels determined by a multidisciplinary planning team using standardized assessment instruments (p. 20). Information from teachers, parents, and the students themselves can be included in an ongoing process of instruction, performance, and reflection. However, the increasing national infatuation with performance assessments, especially portfolios, should not be interpreted as a solution to issues of assessment and minority students. In fact, these assessments may require a more thorough understanding of the content material and the desired student outcomes than conventional standardized measures. A writing portfolio can become merely a collection of writing samples without thoughtful reflection on the nature of writing; how a student is expected to manifest competence in writing; the criteria upon which writing samples will be evaluated.

Camp (1992) suggest a series of questions that might guide the development and use of performance assessments:

The first two questions address *learning and instruction:*

1. What do we want students to learn?

2. What kind of experiences do we think would be most appropriate for them to learn from?

The following questions address issues for *assessment:*

3. How would we know that students are learning what we want them to learn?

4. What kinds of evidence do we believe would be convincing?

5. From what sources and contexts can that evidence be gathered?

Observation and documentation; projects combining instruction and assessment; performances; portfolios; publications and exhibitions; conventional tests or adaptations of them?

6. Who should respond, observe, or evaluate in each case? Classroom teachers; students' peers; teachers in groups or in pairs; parents; supervisors or curriculum coordinators?

7. What criteria should be applied? How might they be developed? How should they be made public?

8. What audiences need to know about student achievement and development?

9. How much and what kind of information would be most useful for each of these audiences? What procedures would invite them to contribute in meaningful ways to the discourse about student learning?

10. What review process would enable us to determine whether

    a. we're getting the kind of information we want

    b. the information serves the purposes most important to each audience

    c. the process of getting the information supports genuine teaching and learning? (pp. 261–62)

Below are a series of prompts employed by Picone-Zocchia (1997) to insure such results.

Portfolio Prompts

1. Choose a piece that you feel best shows you as a creative writer.

2. Select something that shows you can analyze a piece of literature, discussing plot, character, or setting.

3. Choose a piece that you feel shows how well you edit and revise. Explain the steps you went through, and include all drafts.

4. Find a sample that shows how well you communicate orally.

5. Select one story for your portfolio that you could have changed to improve, and explain how you would make those changes.

6. Include two samples of work that you feel show how you've grown as a writer, and explain the differences that you see.

7. Free/Pick—choose one additional piece from any of your work. Explain why you decided to include this in your portfolio.

Name _____ Date _____

Mrs. Zocchia _____ Portfolio Prompt #1 _____

The piece that I feel best shows me as a creative writer is _____

_____. I chose this piece because _____

_____

_____

_____

_____

_____

_____

_____

_____

_____

_____

_____

_____

_____

_____

_____

_____

Name ————————————— Date —————————————

Mrs. Zocchia ——————————— Portfolio Prompt #2 ——————

————————————————————— is an example of something

that shows how well I can analyze a piece of literature. In this piece, I discussed

———————————————————————————————

———————————————————————————————

———————————————————————————————

———————————————————————————————

———————————————————————————————

———————————————————————————————

———————————————————————————————

———————————————————————————————

———————————————————————————————

———————————————————————————————

———————————————————————————————

———————————————————————————————

———————————————————————————————

———————————————————————————————

———————————————————————————————

———————————————————————————————

———————————————————————————————

Name _____ Date _____

Mrs. Zocchia _____ Portfolio Prompt #3 _____

_____ shows what a good editor I can

be and how well I revise my work. There were several things that I had to do.

_____

_____

_____

_____

_____

_____

_____

_____

_____

_____

_____

_____

_____

_____

_____

_____

_____

Name _____ Date _____

Mrs. Zocchia _____ Portfolio Prompt #4 _____

_____ best shows me a public

speaker because _____

_____

_____

_____

_____

_____

_____

_____

_____

_____

_____

_____

_____

_____

_____

_____

Name _____   Date _____

Mrs. Zocchia _____   Portfolio Prompt #5 _____

I wish I had a chance to change _____

which I wrote in _____. If I could, I would _____

_____

_____

_____

_____

_____

_____

_____

_____

_____

_____

_____

_____

_____

_____

Name _____ Date _____

Mrs. Zocchia _____ Portfolio Prompt #6 _____

When I look at _____ and _____ I can

really see my growth as a writer. I've changed in some important ways.

_____

_____

_____

_____

_____

_____

_____

_____

_____

_____

_____

_____

_____

_____

_____

Name _____ Date _____

Mrs. Zocchia _____ Portfolio Prompt #7 _____

For my free pick, I choose_____

because_____

_____

_____

_____

_____

_____

_____

_____

_____

_____

_____

_____

_____

_____

_____

Wesson & King (1996) suggest that there are many advantages to using portfolios. Portfolio assessment is formative assessment that allows both you and your students to monitor their progress over the course of the year. You can thus make timely adjustments in instructional methods.

Portfolios provide a forum for students to assess and reflect on their growth. Typically, standardized assessments are administered at the beginning of the school year and at the end to provide benchmarks of learning. This approach holds little value for special educators. We are concerned about monitoring progress as the year unfolds.

The portfolio model of assessment structures the process for students to assume ownership of their learning, which promotes an internal locus of control. Such an approach encourages students to become invested in their learning by empowering them.

The portfolio model emphasizes breadth and scope of learning, which is a more sensitive model by which to assess learning than is a model focusing on a narrow set of skills.

Yet the potential application of this model in the modern special education classroom is not without some disadvantages. The greatest problem is the issue of time. Teachers are challenged to restructure their time to schedule conferences. During conferences, the actual tasks of collecting materials, sharing them with peers, reflecting on the materials, and evaluating them need to be accomplished.

- The criteria for judging materials need specification and involvement from the student. Clearly, the teacher is the guiding force in pinpointing the standards for evaluating the student's products, but it should be done in collaboration with the learner. Teacher education addressing the specification of these standards is necessary if portfolios are to be used to their potential.

- Teachers must employ a record-keeping system that is time-efficient and meaningful. This certainly can be challenging in light of the already existing time demands facing the special educator. Classroom guides for use in reading/writing instruction in general education would be an excellent starting point to get tips on establishing criteria and record-keeping systems that might prove helpful for exceptional education applications (Farr and Tone, 1994; Tierney, Carter, and Desai, 1991).

- The methodology to encourage the reflection process needs a priori specification so the student can meaningfully reflect on growth. The role of the teacher in assisting the student with this process is best conceptualized as a collaborative/consultative process. The teacher must feel comfortable in the role of getting the student to talk about his or her progress rather than the traditional role of describing and passing judgments about student work without student input.

Though special educators are trained to value student-centered learning, they face an additional challenge in using this model with colleagues in general education who might feel more comfortable with a teacher-centered form of assessment. Thus, for those special educators working closely with general educators, the challenge to adopt this developmental perspective to assessment will be ongoing and require a great deal of in-service and collaborative efforts (p. 45) Their guidelines for developing and using portfolios are:

1. *Both the teacher and the student help compose the portfolio.* The student's ideas about what to include are important, because the portfolio is a chronicle of learning from the learner's and teacher's points of view. However, the teacher may require some additional ideas about items that contribute to an understanding of the student's progress. Thus, the contents are a combination of items selected by the teacher and the student.

2. *The portfolio is a selective collection relating to the school or district instructional goals for the grade.* Not every piece of writing should go into it. If no specific goals are available, then the teacher should develop specific goals. In special education, the individualized education program (IEP) is already in place, therefore, the selection of items to be placed in the portfolio is based on the IEP. Only goal-relevant information needs to be included. Another criterion for selection is the degree to which the item helps the teacher and student make instructional decisions.

3. *The portfolio should be multifaceted and include many different types of data.* It is impossible to represent a student's growth with only one kind of measure; multiple sources of information should be used.

4. *The portfolio should be organized by areas and time.* For example, in a literacy portfolio, reading-related items may be in one section and put in chronological order to show progress. The written-language data could be in the next section and also be in a time series order. An alternative organizational scheme would be to place items that deal with the same thematic unit within a section. For a thematic unit on bears, that section of the portfolio may contain a list of sources used to research bears, rough drafts of the report, and the final copy, as well as bear stories the student read, an audiotape of the student reading a selection from a chosen book, a bear poem written by the student, and a videotape of the Three Bears play put on by the class. There is no one way to organize the portfolio, and the decision of how to organize should be systematic and deliberate on the part of the teacher and student as they discuss the possibilities and decide on a rationale for choosing a specific organizational scheme.

5. *Portfolios should be accessible to both teachers and students so that the information they contain may be used and updated frequently.* Teachers may want to develop a time-line so that at the end of every unit or report card period,

every student's portfolio will be reviewed and items added and deleted. Without a specified time-line, some children's portfolios may remain stagnant and become merely a record-keeping system, as opposed to a link to instruction. An alternative is to update and check one portfolio daily and, thereby, schedule reviews at regular intervals (about monthly) for each student (p. 47–48). (See Appendix A for a report on teachers responses to the use of a developmental scale for rating portfolios)

Parent/Teacher Observation and Interview

The Student Ability Conference. Since no single observer can describe the complete range of an individual's ability and achievement, I propose that an integral part of the assessment process include the dialogue among teachers, parents, and, whenever possible, the student whose academic performance is under scrutiny. I propose the model of a student ability conference in which an open discussion of the student's performance in a specific domain or set of domains is discussed from a variety of perspectives. Such a conference can provide an opportunity to explore strategies to identify and enhance the range of talents that specific children may possess, as well as to isolate academic areas that may require alternate instructional approaches. In addition, the student ability conference can also provide an opportunity for teachers and parents to form a positive educational partnership. This conference is similar to a prereferral meeting or a teacher assistance team meeting discussed previously with the difference being the addition of the student (when appropriate) and parents. (See form below.)

STUDENT ABILITY CONFERENCE

Student's name: <u>Naomi R</u>

Teacher: <u>Mrs. Dunkin</u>   Date: <u>June 22, 1993</u>

Parents: <u>Mr. & Mrs. R</u>

Address: <u>2401 West Main Street, Sayville, NY 11782</u>

Home phone: <u>(516) 374–9001</u>   Work phone: <u>374–2108</u>

Birth: <u>October 11, 1986</u>

Members Present:

Mrs. R., Parent	Dr. Barone, Psychologist
Ms. Dunkin, Teacher	Mr. Jones, Art Teacher
Naomi, Student	Ms. Maldora, Nurse
Ms. Abrams, Social Worker	Dr. Alegro, Principal

Summary

Mrs. R. reports that Naomi is a responsible child at home, assisting with her siblings and is very cooperative. School personnel report the same. Mr. Jones, the art teacher, believes that Naomi has exceptional talent in art and this should be pursued through an enrichment program. Dr. Barone, the school psychologist, agreed and noted that her visual—motor skills were superior, but he was concerned about her reading skills. Mrs. R. is also concerned about this as was Mrs. Dunkin her teacher. Naomi also feels uncomfortable reading in class and doesn't understand why she can't read. It was agreed that Ms. Abrams, the school social worker would meet with Naomi and the reading teacher to conduct a brief reading evaluation and then schedule another student ability conference in two weeks to discuss the findings.

Evidence of Achievement Must be Gathered over Time and in a Variety of Contexts

A major concern in the educational assessment of urban students is the speed with which such an intrinsically complicated task is expected to be accomplished. In fact, the rush to classify students, which has led to an increase in the number of ill-trained educational evaluators, is based more on a desire to avoid litigation resulting from being found "out of compliance" with state and local regulations than on theoretically and ethically sound assessment practices. While there are very real pressures placed on urban school districts, it must also be acknowledged that significant numbers of students are classified in special education categories, not because evaluators truly believe that their assessment has revealed some neurologically based learning problem, which would preclude normal academic development given the best possible conditions, but rather, because the bureaucratic and fiscal constraints of the educational system require classification in order to receive the even most minor support services.

The assessment of atypical learners in urban areas may, in some cases, require a longitudinal assessment of the student's demonstration of ability and achievement in which various interventions are interwoven. As Leung (1996) notes "slowing down" the process can be invaluable. In such case, diagnostic teaching may be necessary to provide a more informative picture of the ways in which a specific student represents knowledge within the context of his or her own experiences. Given the controversy surrounding the theoretical and operational definitions of specific learning disabilities, the most appropriate course of action might well be the careful documentation of the student's learning of new information over a span of time and in a variety of contexts and under varying conditions. (See Appendix B for an example of such a process for mathematics and science development.)

Evidence of Student Performance Must be Based on Curriculum Materials and Experiences that are Familiar to the Student

When the outcome of an assessment will be whether or not to label the student in a special education classification, it is especially important that the assessment of academic achievement be curriculum-based. That is, the assessment of academic achievement should be based on curriculum content that is known to have been taught to the student and on experiences that are not foreign to the student. Large-scale achievement testing rests on the assumption that there is a common core of information being taught to all students, at the same time, in their academic careers. However, it is increasingly apparent that many urban communities are inhabited by children who have temporary residences, such as shelters for the homeless or the battered, and who may not have been able to follow a consistent academic curriculum since they move from residence to residence and from school to school. The inability to ensure a match between material tested and material taught is a serious threat to the validity of the interpretation of test results of such an educational assessment. This goes beyond the use of curriculum measures as discussed by Tucker (1985) to include these additional environmental variables.

Some advantages of curriculum-based assessment are (Grossman 1996):

- It avoids the problem of assessing students on tasks, skills, and knowledge they have not been taught.

- It does not compare students to norms based on a national sample of students, many of whom attend schools that do not resemble theirs and live in other parts of the country.

- Since it can be administered informally as part of the regular classroom activities, it may make students less anxious and thereby provide a more accurate measurement of their achievement.

- It can be used repeatedly with students, whereas standardized tests have to be administered sparingly because they usually do not come in many alternate forms.

- It is more sensitive to short-term improvement in student achievement and provides information that can be used to make day-to-day instructional decisions.

Ysseldyke and Algozzone (1995) also note the value of curriculum-based assessment.

Curriculum-based assessment, when conducted properly, can be an important tool for teachers and diagnostic specialists in a number of ways.

- *Analysis of the learning environment.* By careful examination of the learning environment, curriculum-based assessment helps to identify pitfalls that may be interfering with the student's learning. Such assessment isolate problems with the instructional materials, with the ways in which the manner of presentation (such as lecture or workbook), and with the grouping of students in the classroom.

- *Analysis of task-approach strategies.* By focusing on the student's task-approach strategies, curriculum-based assessment helps teachers identify basic learning skills that the student may need to develop.

- *Examination of student's products.* Through systematic examination of a student's work samples, curriculum-based assessment can spot particular error patterns.

- *Controlling and arranging student tasks.* By manipulating the ways in which materials are presented and the specific tasks that students are asked to perform, the curriculum-based assessment procedure helps teachers determine which approaches are most productive.

Choate, Bennett, Enright, Miller, Poteet, and Rakes (1987) list several reasons for using curriculum-based assessment:

- It complies with the procedural requirements of Public Law 94–142 for assessing students in need of special education.

- It is efficient.

- It is a valid, reliable basis for making decisions.

- It can be used to make different kinds of decisions (for example, screening, program effectiveness).

- It increases student's achievement.

- It helps teachers decide what to teach.

Below is an example of a curriculum-based reading comprehension strategy checklist. It was developed by Howell and Morehead (1987):

A. Active Reading

		Yes	No	Don't know	Adequate	Instruction needed	Additional testing needed
1. Recognizes that reading is an active process of combining prior knowledge with text	1.1 Approaches text with questions and attempts to answer questions						
	1.2 Seeks to clarify meaning						
	1.3 Uses prior knowledge where appropriate						
	1.4 Evaluates arguments, assertions, and proposals in text						
	1.5 Uses cognitive maps to anticipate and analyze text structure						
2. Understands the purpose(s) of reading and that print can be used to convey information, such as the answer to questions	2.1 Reads with expression or automaticity						
	2.2 Adjusts reading rate for material that is not understood						
	2.3 Does not make frequent whole word substitutions and insertions that seem graphically or phonemically similar to the passage word but violate passage meaning						

A. Active Reading *(continued)*

		Yes	No	Don't know	Adequate	Instruction needed	Additional testing needed
	2.4 Is more likely to recall important passage details, not trivial ones						
	2.5 Answers comprehension questions in terms of stated information in passage, not only prior knowledge						

B. Comprehension Monitoring

		Yes	No	Don't know	Adequate	Instruction needed	Additional testing needed
1. Monitors own comprehension of the passage by recognizing when the passage does not make sense or is losing understanding of the passage	1.1 Self-corrects reading errors that violate the meaning of the passage (such as nonmeaningful insertions)						
	1.2 Rereads confusing portions of material, or adjusts reading rate on difficult sections						
	1.3 Can predict upcoming events in the passage						
	1.4 Identifies when additional information is needed, or specifically what kind of information is needed to answer questions						
	1.5 Does not make nonmeaningful insertion errors						

C. Problem Solving

		Yes	No	Don't know	Adequate	Instruction needed	Additional testing needed
1. Uses problem solving to deal with difficult material	1.1 "Where did I get lost?"						
	1.2 "What kind of information would would help me?"						
	1.3 "Where can I find out more?"						
	1.4 "What do the words mean?"						
	1.5 "What relationship has been established?"						
	1.6 "What information belongs with specific characters or concepts?"						
	1.7 "If I understood this what would I know (or be able to do)?"						
2. Discriminates relevant information in the passage by recognizing portions critical to the central meaning of the passage	2.1 Answers "best title" and main idea questions accurately						
	2.2 Retells story with emphasis on major points						
	2.3 Describes author's purpose for writing						
	2.4 Can locate information in the passage that answers assigned questions						

D. Study Skills

		Yes	No	Don't know	Adequate	Instruction needed	Additional testing needed
1. Uses active search skills	1.1 Can describe a search procedure such as multipass						
	1.2 Employs a search procedure at an automatic level						
2. Can paraphrase and summarize	2.1 States key ideas in own words						
	2.2 Follows text structure to restate and summarize						

Evaluators Must be Able to Accept Lack of Closure

As stated previously, the complex nature of the process of accurately identifying children with specific learning disabilities in culturally and linguistically diverse settings is a complicated task that should not be held to the constraints of a traditional assessment. The multiple forms of evidence discussed above and the suggested longitudinal nature of the assessment process are based on the realization that situations will arise in which it is simply not clear that the student's underachievement is a result of inherent processing deficits. In fact, when issues of language, culture, and experience are present, the assessment should not be expected to be simple. Even a thorough assessment can result in confusion as to the existence of a specific learning disability. In such cases, the assessment process should continue, and data should continue to be collected from a variety of sources and in a variety of contexts.

Evaluation, the process of describing student behavior and coming to a decision regarding a level of student performance or a stage of development, should be thoughtful and reflective. Too often the process becomes simply the administration of a set of standardized tests and the interpretation of the resulting set of scores. Two stages, documentation and assessment, must precede any evaluation or judgments made regarding student achievement.

The first process is *documentation* of student learning. This is the process of describing an activity, a behavior, or an interaction in order to understand and later interpret that activity, behavior, or interaction. Just as an ethnographer describes a foreign culture, educators must come to understand the value of description in understanding student behavior. In several school-based research projects, the authors have found that one of the most difficult tasks for teachers is to simply describe student behavior or a specific task without making any judgments. Reporting exactly what has happened, who said what to whom, and under what circumstances is not as simple as it seems. We are all inclined immediately to place our own interpretation on an event. Spradly (1979) reported the following example from the *Minneapolis Tribune:*

CROWD MISTAKES RESCUE ATTEMPT, ATTACKS POLICE

Nov. 23, 1973. Hartford, Connecticut. Three policemen giving a heart massage and oxygen to a heart attack victim Friday were attacked by a crowd of 75 to 100 persons who apparently did not realize what the police were doing.

Other policemen fended off the crowd of mostly Spanish speaking residents until an ambulance arrived. Police said they tried to explain to the crowd what they were doing, but the crowd apparently thought they were beating the woman.

Despite the policeman's efforts, the victim . . . died.

From the above example it is easy to see how each of us brings our own cultural experiences to an interpretation. It often takes enormous restraint to look at a behavior or an interaction, realize that multiple interpretations are possible, and withhold judgment. Very often we see the inclination of teachers to report that the student "did well"; "felt comfortable"; or "was not trying very hard." If we are to get an accurate picture of student performance, the educational staff must recognize the importance of descriptions of student activities. The ability to provide accurate descriptions in documenting student behaviors also allows educational staff to understand what occurred and to bring their own interpretations to the situation without prejudice.

As a documentation system, the *Primary Language Record: Handbook for Teachers* (Heinemann, 1988) and *Patterns of Learning* (Center for Language for Primary Education, 1990) are extremely helpful. These two documentation systems, designed in England, include input from parents, children, and teachers. In addition, a variety of contexts and academic areas are considered. See Table 3.1.

Table 3.1
Primary Language Record

Academic Areas	CONTEXTS		
	Student	Sociocultural	Instructional
Reasoning			
Language (comprehension)			
Speech production			
Reading			
Writing			
Mathematics			

Second, the *assessment* of student learning. I use Salvia and Ysseldyke's 1995 definition of assessment: *"the process of collecting data for the purpose of (1) specifying and verifying problems and (2) making decisions about students"* (p. 5). The guiding principles for a model of educational assessment have been outlined above:

1. Clear definition of the purpose of the assessment

2. Diagnostic question must guide the assessment

3. Multiple forms of evidence of student performance must be gathered

4. Evidence of achievement must be gathered over time and in a variety of contexts

5. Evidence of student performance must be based on curriculum materials and experiences that are familiar to the student

6. Evaluators must be able to accept lack of closure

It is important to underscore that I define assessment as a process in which pertinent evidence is collected in a systematic manner.

Finally, once student behavior has been described and multiple forms of evidence have been gathered over time, an *evaluation* of student progress may be made in order to make decisions or to classify the level of performance. It is at this level that I begin to make hard decisions that may result in a special education classification. It is also at this level that I can reevaluate the documentation and assessment process to determine if there is enough relevant information to allow an informed decision to be made.

Examples of Alternative Assessment Systems

US DOE-funded Alternative Assessment Project. *Alternative Special Education Assessment of Urban Minority Students* was a pilot study in which a group of urban elementary teachers designed initial literacy performance assessments appropriate for urban minority students identified under special education headings as well as for regular education students. A researcher met weekly with groups of special and regular education teachers. Major outcomes of the work were the finding 1) that teachers need long-term and ongoing support in the design and administration of performance assessments, 2) that the communication between general and regular education teachers needs to be facilitated when there is ongoing conversation around samples of student work, and 3) that the school-based evaluation process requires dialogue among a variety of professionals who have very different perspectives on and definitions of student progress. See Table 3.2.

Table 3.2
Summary of 1991–1992 Reading Evaluation/Assessment

Student reader: _____ Student's grade: _____

Teacher: _____

Dates of reading performance samples: from:_____ to: _____

Is English the student's only language? ____Y ____N

    If no, what other language is spoken? _____

    In what language(s) was the reading done? _____

Check Sampling Procedures	
Miscue analysis	
Running record	
Individual conference	
Group discussion	
Writing/drawing sample	
Other (describe)	

Table 3.2 (continued)
Performance Evaluation

Level	Instructional/ Functional			Grade Equivalent		
Traits	Strongly evident (3)	Emergent (2)	Not evident (1)	Strongly evident (3)	Emergent (2)	Not evident (1)
Reader comprehends text						
Reader uses variety of strategies when reading aloud						
Reader self-reflections on own reading progress						

Standard Test Scores

Test	Age Score	Grade Score	Standard Score	Percentile

Summary of Writing Assessment Evaluation 1991–1992

Student writer: _____ Student's grade: _____

Teacher _____

Dates of performance samples: from: _____ to: _____

Is English the student's only language? _____Y _____N

    If no, what other language is spoken? _____

Are samples in student's dominant language? _____Y _____N

    If not, in what language(s) are the writings? _____

Table 3.2 (continued)
Summary of Writing Assessment Evaluation 1991–1992

Writing samples consist of:

Drafts and extracts _____   Final versions _____

Lists _____   Letters _____

Stories _____   Poems _____

Personal writings _____   Expository writings _____

Other: _____

Performance Evaluation

Level	Instructional/ Functional			Grade Equivalent		
Traits	Strongly evident (3)	Emergent (2)	Not evident (1)	Strongly evident (3)	Emergent (2)	Not evident (1)
Writer's meaning conveyed to reader						
Mastery of spelling conventions						
Mastery of Conventions (mechanics)						
Focused approach to the writing						
Writer is self-reflective						

Standardized Test Scores

Test	Age	Grade	Standard Score	Percentile

The board of education of South Brunswick, New Jersey, has been involved in the development of a portfolio culture for their schools for some time. As part of this process, a stage level of literacy development has been developed and a series of assessments have been designed to assist teachers in identifying competence at each level. See figure 3.1.

Figure 3.1 K-2 South Brunswick School District Reading/Writing Scale (Draft 5) Development of Children's Strategies for Making Sense of Print

---

Level 1: Early Emergent

Displays an awareness of some convention of reading, such as front/back of books, distinctions between print and pictures. Sees the construction of meaning from text as "magical" or exterior to the print. While the child may be interested in the contents of books, there is as yet little apparent attention to turning written marks into language. Is beginning to notice environmental print.

Level 2: Advanced Emergent

Engages in pretend reading and writing. Uses readinglike ways that clearly approximate book language. Demonstrates a sense of the story being "read," using picture clues and recall of story line. May draw upon predictable language patterns in anticipating (and recalling) the story. Attempts to use letters in writing, sometimes in random or scribble fashion.

Level 3: Early Beginning Reader

Attempts to "really read." Indicates beginning sense of one-to-one correspondence and concept of word. Predicts actively in new material, using syntax and story line. Small stable sight vocabulary is becoming established. Evidence of initial awareness of beginning and ending sounds, especially in invented spelling.

Level 4: Advanced Beginning Reader

Starts to draw on major cue systems; self-corrects or identifies words through use of letter-sound patterns, sense of story, or syntax. Reading may be laborious especially with new material, requiring considerable effort and some support. Writing and spelling reveal awareness of letter patterns and conventions of writing such as capitalization and periods.

Level 5: Early Independent Reader

Handles familiar material on own, but still needs some support with unfamiliar material. Figures out words and self-corrects by drawing on a combination of letter-sound relationships, word structure, story line, and syntax. Strategies of rereading or of guessing from larger chunks of texts are becoming well established. Has a large stable sight vocabulary. Conventions of writing are understood.

Level 6: Advanced Independent Reader

Reads independently, using multiple strategies flexibly. Monitors and self-corrects for meaning. Can read and understand most material when the content is appropriate. Conventions of writing and spelling are—for the most part—under control.

Reading Samples

Student's name _____

Date of the sample: _____

Is English the child's only language? _____Y _____N

    If no, what other language is spoken? _____

Is the reading in the child's dominant language? _____Y _____N

- *This reading represents:*

    an oral reading sample _____

    a silent reading sample _____

- *The reading is a:*

    Book _____ Story ____ Poem ____ Letter ____ Personal ____

Sampling Procedure Used

Miscue analysis _____Running record _____

Individual conference _____ Group discussion _____

Writing/drawing sample _____

Other (describe) _____

Reading Samples (*continued*)

Context of the Reading

- The reading was self-chosen: _____Y _____N
- The reading was assigned: _____Y _____N

Evaluation of the Reading

Child reads with ease and confidence: _____

Child reads with assistance: _____

	Some evidence	Little evidence	Teacher's comments
Child's Response to the Text *personal response *critical response (understands, evaluates, appreciates wider meanings)			

	Some evidence	Little evidence	Teacher's comments
Child's Comprehension of the Material Read			

	Some evidence	Little evidence	Teacher's comments
Strategies Used When Reading Aloud			(provide examples)
Draws on previous experience to make sense of the book/text			
Plays at reading			
Uses book language			
Reads pictures			
Focuses on print (directionality, 1:1 correspondence, recognition of certain words)			
Uses semantic/ syntactic/ grapho-phonic cues			
Uses prediction			
Self-corrects			
Uses several strategies			

	Some evidence	Little evidence	Teacher's comments
Child's Reflections on His/Her Own Reading			

	Some evidence	Little evidence	Teacher's comments
Teacher's Reflections on Child's Reading Progress			
What does this reading show about the child's general development as a reader?			
How does this reading fit into the range of the child's previous reading?			
What experience or support is needed to insure further reading development?			

Writing Samples

Student's name _____

Date of the sample: _____

Is English the child's only language? _____Y _____N

    If no, what other language is spoken? _____

Is the writing in the child's dominant language? _____Y _____N

If not, in what other language is the writing? _____Y _____N

- *This writing represents:*

    a draft _____

    or

    a final version _____

    an extract from a larger sample of writing _____

    or

    a complete piece of text _____

- The writing is a:

List_____ Letter_____ Story_____ Poem_____

Personal writing _____ Expository writing _____

Context of the Writing
- The topic was self-chosen _____ Y _____ N
- The writing was assigned _____ Y _____ N
- The child wrote alone _____ Y _____ N
- The writing was done in collaboration with others _____ Y _____ N
- Other children were involved in editing the writing _____ Y _____ N

	Some evidence	Little evidence	Teacher's comments
How Did the Child Approach the Writing? *The child was absorbed in the writing *What was the child's response to suggestions?			
Reader's Response to the Writing The writer's intent is conveyed to the reader			

	Some evidence	Little evidence	Teacher's comments
Development of spelling and conventions of writing			(provide examples)
*Spelling strategies classified as:			
auditory approximations			
visual approximations			
generally good guesses			
ufo's (untelligible spellings)			
(Give Examples)			
Conventions:			
*What do you notice from this writing about the child's awareness of:			
the layout of different kinds of:			
texts			
punctuation of written language			

	Some evidence	Little evidence	Teacher's comments
Child's Reflections			
Teacher's Reflections What does this writing show about the child's development as a writer? How does the writing fit into the range of the child's previous writing (motivation, spelling, composition)? What experience or support is needed to insure further development?			

4

Interventions

Assessment is a means to an end. The end result is the development and implementation of an intervention plan. The interventions provded in this text would be insufficient for the novice teacher. The beginning teacher should consult the numerous textbooks that deal specifically with methods and materials for students with special educational needs. Some recommended texts are:

Bos, C. S. and Vaughan, S. (1994) *Strategies for teaching students with learning and behavior problems* (3rd ed.). Boston: Allyn and Bacon.

Deshler, D. D., Ellis, E. S. and Lenz, B. K. (1996) *Teaching adolescents with learning disabilities: Strategies and methods* (2nd ed.). Denver: Love Publishing Co.

Mercer, C. R., and Mercer, A. (1996) *Teaching students with learning problems* (3rd ed.). Columbus, Ohio: Merrill.

Polloway, E. A. and Patton, J. R. (1996) *Strategies for teaching learners with special needs* (6th ed.). Columbus, OH: Merrill.

An intervention plan must be based on results from a thorough, sound, valid, and reliable psychoeducational assessment. The clinical teaching model proposed by Lerner (1993) requires continual decision-making on the part of the teacher. The phases of the process are:

1. assessment

2. planning

3. implementation

4. evaluation

5. modification of assessment

6. continuation of steps 1–5

As noted previously, this is an ongoing process that enables the teacher to make reasonable decisions and modify instruction according to student performance. The assessment model proposed in this text leads to the development of a remediation plan that follows the clinical teaching model, but also considers the nature and needs of a culturally and linguistically diverse population. However, caution must be used when interpreting any finding. The results of the psychoeducational assessment must be taken as hypotheses. This is not factual information. Once hypotheses have been formulated, we teach the student and determine whether to affirm or reject the hypotheses. This is an ongoing process of teaching-testing-teaching. The instructional process must be guided by principles that govern our practice (Gearhart, 1985). The principles most appropriate for the population of learning disabled students who reside in urban settings are discussed below.

Principles of Instruction

1. *There is no single "right" method to be used with learning disabled students.* Approaches to instruction for learning disabled students are chosen on the basis of what they need to learn, how they learn best, and what strategies are necessary (Smith, 1995). To suggest that all learning disabled students who happen to be African-American be taught one way and all learning disabled students who happen to speak Spanish as their native language should be taught a different specific way would be foolhardy. Equally as foolhardy is the noting that all learning disabled students should be taught one way. As Smith (1995) notes, the individual needs of each learning disabled student should to be considered when developing an appropriate instructional plan.

2. *All other factors being equal, the newest (to the student) method should be used.* It is not unusual for some students to have experienced failure with the same techniques for a number of years. This is particularly true in parts of our country where the financial resources for schools has not been forthcoming. Same methods, same materials, same failure-ridden experiences. By providing a novel approach / methods / materials to the student, the teacher can motivate them and reverse their negativity toward learning.

3. *Some type of positive reconditioning should be implemented.* For many students failure has been a significant part of their school experience. These

students must be provided with strong, consistent, positive reinforcement for all their efforts, not merely completion of a task. "Love of learning" is not intrinsically motivating for many students because most of their efforts have not yielded results. Therefore, some type of external reinforcement must be employed, especially during the early stages of learning.

4. *The existence of nonspecific or difficult-to-define disabilities must be recognized, particularly in older students.* Often educators are over concerned with causation. It is not unusual to be unable to cite a specific causative factor in many learning disabled students, especially in cases where there is a diverse population, limited support services in the schools, and cultural and linguistic differences. To withhold services because of a lack of a specific, readily identifiable cause would be a great disservice. Emphasis should be placed on the current functioning of the student and instructional methods that will reduce the gap between potential and performance.

5. *Complete, accurate information about learning strengths and weakness is essential.* As previously noted, a thorough psychoeducational assessment, as proposed in the previous chapter, is essential. Without such information the remediation plan will be ill defined and haphazard. With it, a specific intervention plan can be developed, implemented, and monitored.

6. *Educational time and effort must be carefully maximized for the student with learning disabilities.* Class size is increasing and financial resources are decreasing in urban centers throughout the United States. This makes it even more critical to insure well thought-out programs that are carefully monitored and modified if necessary. Teachers must be competent in data collection procedures that enable them to make timely educational decisions so that students' time in school is time well spent.

The six principles cited above will govern all instruction. One mechanism for connecting such instructional services is the Individualized Educational Program (IEP). It's major components will be discussed below.

Individualized Educational Program (IEP)

Bigge (1988) suggests that "the IEP is a major vehicle for translating assessment results into instructional objectives for students requiring special education" (p. 28). The IEP must include:

1. The student's current level of performance in the areas of concern.

2. Annual and short-term objectives.

3. The specific education services to be provided and the extent to which the student will participate in regular education.

4. The projected date for initiation of the program and anticipated duration of such services.

5. A description of the schedule and evaluation procedures for determining whether objectives are being met.

An example of "typical" IEP used in the state of New York is presented below:

INDIVIDUALIZED EDUCATION PLAN

I.D. #: _____ CSE Date: _____

Background/Current Placement

Student's Name: _____ D.O.B.: _____ G.A.: _____

Parent's Name: _____

Address: _____

Telephone: (H) _____ (W) _____

Student's dominant language: _____ Home language: _____

Current school: _____ Grade: _____

Program: _____

CSE Recommendations

Nature of meeting: _____ Initial _____ Annual review _____ Triennial _____ Other review

Classification: _____

Placement: _____ North Side _____ Willets Road _____ Wheatly _____ Other (specify below)

_____

Program: _____ Related services _____ Resource room _____ Special class _____ Other _____

Individualized Education Plan *(continued)*

Class size: _____ Carnegie credits to date: _____

Specialized transportation: _____

Specialized equipment: _____

Twelve-month program: _____ Yes_____ No   (site):_____

Regular phys. ed. program: _____ Yes _____ No

Adaptive phys. ed. _____ Yes _____ No

Foreign language waiver: _____ Yes _____ No

Other waivers: _____

Transitional/Declassification support: _____

Testing Modifications

_____ None _____ Extended time _____ Special location

_____ Use of calculator _____ Questions/directions _____ Braille/large type

_____ Dictation of answers (use of tape recorder, word processor, or other)

_____ No penalty for spelling except on spelling tests

_____ Other: _____

Description of Educational Services

Percentage of day mainstreamed _____

Percentage of day in special services _____

Svcs/class/res. rm.	Amount per day	Days per week	Person responsible

IEP (*continued*)   Name: _____

Present Level of Educational Performance/Function Levels

Area	Name of Test	Date	Level
Reading-dec.			
Reading comp.			
Mathematics			
Written language			
Spelling			
Other			
Other			

Classroom functioning/least restrictive environment statement: _____

_____

Learning Characteristics

Cognitive functioning: _____

Learning style: Modality strengths and weaknesses: _____

Recommended strategies: _____

Management Needs

_____ Classroom behavior does not interfere with instruction

_____ Classroom behavior may interfere with instruction

_____ Aggressive, self-abusive, withdrawn, or other behaviors requiring highly intensive supervision

_____ Severe impairment requiring habitation, treatment, and intensive monitoring

Comments: _____

_____

IEP *(continued)*   Name: _____

Social Development

Vision: _____ Normal _____ Needs corrective lenses _____ Vision impairment _____ Blind

Hearing: _____ Normal _____ Mild loss _____ Hearing impairment _____ Deaf

Current medications/treatments: _____

Special alerts/comments: _____

Educational Plan

Date of initial classification: _____

Projected date of begin this plan: _____

Current plan runs from _____ to _____

Projected date of review: _____

Evaluation criteria: _____

Annual Goals	Short-Term Objective

Committee on Special Educational Attendance

Committee members

Chairperson: _____

Psychologist: _____

Physician (if requested): _____

Parent member: _____

L.D. specialist: _____

Speech/lang. pathologist _____

Counselor: _____

Others in attendance

Teacher(s) _____

Reading teachers: _____

Parents: _____

Student: _____

Others: _____

For the special educator concerned with remediation, the most critical elements are the annual goals and the short-term instructional objectives. They provide a bridge between assessment and instruction.

Writing Annual Goals and Short-Term Instructional Objectives

Annual goals are general statements that form the outline of the IEP. Thompson (1977) believes that five components are necessary to provide adequate information:

a. direction of change desired

b. deficit of excess

c. present level

d. expected level

e. resources needed/expected level

He provides examples:

1. Direction of change desired can be stated as: increase (reading ability, running speed, speed fluency, etc.), decrease (math errors, time off tasks, absences, etc.), maintain (on-task behavior, attention span, motor control, etc.).

2. Deficit or excess is the general area needing special attention. For example, a student may have a deficit in receptive language, expressive language, and reading, or peer relationship, ability to attend to task, and so on. Examples of excessive behavior might include: physical aggressiveness, talking out, anxiety level, etc. You *increase* behavior in the area of deficit and *decrease* behavior in the area of excess.

3. The present level is a description of what the student currently does in the area of deficit or excess. It may also be called the current level or performance. For example, current level or reading, naming numbers to 20, using two-word utterances, ability to stay on task, etc.

4. Expected level is where you reasonably think the child will be, given the appropriate resources. You must decide on the time parameters: it could be a year, a month, or a few weeks. The statement should be dealing with a general area of change and predicted level of performance, such as:

• reading at grade-two level

• speaking in three-word utterances

• comprehending three-step oral constructs

The expected level must be based on the needs of the specific student. These levels will vary from student to student. To write that all of your students will be ready or at a particular grade level at the end of the year would not make a great deal of sense. Rather, based on the needs of the student, the current level of functions, where do you expect him/her to be in the future (weeks, months, years)?

5. Resources needed would be specialists, material, methods, settings, etc. For example, special therapy would be considered a resource (or currently called a related service) or parent training, counseling, a particular piece of equipment, etc. The five elements follow a sequence from:

Direction > deficit / excess > from (level___) to (level___) and resources necessary.

An example would be: Increase reading readiness from preprimer to primer level, using individual and small group instruction and parent tutoring, emphasizing a language-based approach.

Short-Term Behavioral Objectives. These should follow from and be consistent with the annual goals. Short-term behavioral objectives are much more precise than annual goals. They should include the following components:

1. performance

2. conditions

3. standard or level of performance

The following examples are provided by Thompson (1977):

1. The first component needed is the *performance,* or what the child is to do. The performance should be specific, identifying a task that can be achieved in a short time. Examples are:

unties and ties shoelace

says numbers to 20

identifies vowel sounds

orders letters of the alphabet

washes dishes

walks twenty feet

These are small segments of behavior and should be manageable units of instruction. Depending on the degree of handicap, the desired performance may have to be divided into smaller segments. Instead of stating, write numbers, as the behavior; you might be more concerned with such performance elements as identifies pencil, identifies paper, holds pencil, draws straight line, draws circle. The size, or difficulty, of the behavior stated is determined by the needs and characteristics of the child. The person carrying out the instruction must judge the appropriateness of instructional segments.

2. The next component is the condition of the performance.

What are the circumstances surrounding the performance?

Are any environmental factors relevant?

Can reference material be used?

Does he or she have more than one trial?

Are there time limitations?

Does he or she perform alone? With a group?

Is the performance oral, written, or a demonstration?

Does he or she have any choice of conditions?

Is special equipment needed?

Can he or she utilize the advice of other students?

Is there anything unique about the material?

Are the circumstances real or are they contrived?

Examples of conditions are:

given fifty addition facts

without the aid of cane or crutches

provided with the necessary equipment

without the aid of tutors

using a standard typewriter

using a hearing aid

given ten color cards

placed in a mock-up of a stockroom situation

given standard household cleaning tools

3. The next element needed in an STO is the level of performance expected, or the *standard* of performance. *How well* is the child supposed to do something? Examine the following phrases:

at least ninety percent correct

with no more than six spelling errors per paragraph

according to the rules

sportsmanlike in the opinion of the opposing team

at least eighty percent out of the fifty correctly

as judged by a qualified observer

accurate to two decimal places

at least six consecutive correct trials

according to accepted standards

according to the directions in the manual

with no pauses or redundancies

The standard is often determined by the nature of the task, because complete mastery of one task may be necessary for learning the next one. Counting to ten is necessary before you can count to twenty. You have to be able to walk before you can run. Writing letters must precede writing words. *In cases where the standard of performance is understood to be a hundred percent, it doesn't need to be stated, or it can be stated as done "correctly."* To "tie shoes correctly" is easily understood. To "tie shoes in three minutes" makes sense because speed of performance may be a factor; the task is understood to be performed with a hundred percent accuracy.

If the standard is not clearly understood to be a hundred percent, then it should be stated. Examples of performance standards are with eighty percent accuracy. Completed in five minutes, at least twenty times, and leaving no waste. How well should a child do something? Ask yourself and write down the answer.

Specificity. How specific or detailed should the statement be? It is both impractical and foolish to write a statement such as: Given a sharpened, 4-inch, no. 2 lead pencil, a sheet of yellow 8½-by-11 inch paper with lines spaces ⅝ inch apart, and ten 3-by-5 inch cards with a single number written on each to serve as a model, the child will correctly copy the numbers.

It is sufficient to state: Correctly copy numbers 1–10.

The statement implies a writing tool, something on which to write, and a model from which to copy.

Simplicity with completeness is the combination needed, with the purpose of communicating effectively. Short-term objectives should communicate what the child is to do (performance), the circumstances of the performance (conditions), and how well he or she is to perform (standard), but the three components are not always specifically stated. Their performance is always stated, but conditions or standards may be implied. However, the implication should be very clear. When in doubt, include the component in the statement.

Another question relating to specificity is the degree to which very small units of instruction are stated as objectives. There is no simple rule to follow, which will solve that problem for teachers. They must rely on their professional judgment to make the question less important as an obstacle.

If teachers stated specific objectives for every element of instruction for every child, there would be no time to teach. Attempts have been made to produce what is called a "task analysis" for specific areas of instruction, such as arithmetic, reading, and social skills.

The IEP should be viewed as a valuable planning tool. The special educator must develop reasonable and sensible annual goals and short-term behavioral objectives, if this document is to be employed to guide instruction. Figure 4.1 (Thompson, 1977) summarizes the major components of each.

Figure 4.1 Characteristics of LTOs and STOs

LTO's have five components: direction deficit/excess, present level (from), expected level (to), and resources.	STOs have three components: performance, conditions, and standards.
All five are present in nearly every instance. ("Maintain" may be a special case.)	Performance is always stated. Standard may be assumed in some cases. Conditions are sometimes implied.
LTOs are written on the basis of the assessment data, prior to placement.	STOs flow from LTOs, are consistent with them, and are written after placement.
LTOs are broad in nature and and over longer periods of time.	STOs are concerned with small units of behavior and should be attainable in a short time.
LTOs state what will be evaluated.	STOs provide a record for use in evaluation.

Task Analysis. Breaking tasks down into their various components is critical for the teaching of students with special needs, regardless of the ethnic/racial background, the socioeconomic status, or the cultural and linguistic diversity of the population served. All students benefit from this type of instruction. Siegel and Gold (1982) note that teachers of learning disabled students must be competent in (1) selecting a relevant and appropriate task, (2) creating a specific sequence of steps based on the hierarchy of competencies necessary to perform that task, and (3) making the necessary modifications based on the student's strengths and weaknesses. They provide the following examples:

Multiplying a Two-Place Number by a One-Place Number

Behavioral Objective. When given ten multiplication examples (written) of a two-placed multiplicand by a one-place multiplier, five of which require "carrying," in e.g., 75 24, the pupil will be able to do them.

$$x3, \ x2$$

Entering Behavior. Knowledge of the multiplication tables (not perfectly), place value, how to multiply such examples without "carrying" (from prior experience in addition).

Sequential components

1. from use of special "multiplication-addition" cards to no cards. (Although the pupil has prior knowledge of the concept that multiplication is really a special case of addition, this visual prompt may assist him or her in multiplication):

$$
\begin{array}{cccc}
32 & 32 & & \\
\underline{x4} & 32 & 75 & 75 \\
 & 32 & \underline{x3} & 75 \\
 & \underline{+32} & & \underline{+75}
\end{array}
$$

2. from easier numbers to harder numbers:

   a) from no "carrying" to "carrying"

   b) from easy tables (e.g., 2, 3, 4, 5) to harder ones (e.g., 6, 7, 8)

   c) from examples necessitating adding within decades to those requiring closing the tens (e.g., 24+4 to 28+5)

   d) from the easier form of communication to the harder form (e.g., 35 + 2 to 32 + 5)

3. from illustrative examples on display to none

4. from multiplication matrix chart available to none

5. from graph paper (large spaced) to unlined paper

6. from memory box

$$48 \\ \underline{\times\ 3}$$

to memory

7. from color coding tens and ones to none

8. from verbal cues (e.g., "start with the ones") to none

9. from regrouping, e.g.,

$$76 \qquad 70 \qquad 6 \\ \underline{\times\ 4}\ =\ \underline{\times\ 4}\ +\ \underline{\times\ 4}$$

to traditional format

10. from materials (e.g., dimes and pennies, squared materials) to numbers

11. from placing an *x* marking the beginning space of the product to none

12. from the teacher and pupil verbalizing the entire example (in unison) to working from memory

13. from drill in determining whether or not a given example requires "carrying" to none

14. from computing the addition portion in writing to doing it mentally

Instructional Procedure

1. Give the pupil several "easy tables" multiplication involving no "carrying": e.g.,

$$32 \qquad 43 \qquad 22 \\ \underline{\times\ 3,} \quad \underline{\times\ 2,} \quad \underline{\times\ 4,}$$

appropriate multiplication/addition cards for reference; a multiplication matrix chart is available throughout; the pupil recites the procedural steps in unison with the teacher (following the demonstration and explanation).

2. Give the pupil several cards involving "carrying" gradually proceeding from easier to harder numbers. Provide a memory box. Matrix chart is still available and continue with unison recitation.

3. As the examples get more difficult, allow the pupil to use written computation for the additional portion:

$$\begin{array}{cc} 6 & \\ 79 & 49 \\ \underline{x\ 7} & \underline{+\ 6} \end{array} \quad < \text{pupil writes}$$

Continue as in step 2.

4. Provide special drill in determining, by inspection, whether or not given examples require "carrying."

5. Same as 3, but fade out the use of the multiplication/addition cards.

6. Same as 5, but fade out the memory box.

7. Same as 6, but fade out matrix chart.

8. Same as 7, but pupil now computes the addition portion mentally.

9. Same as 8, but fade out the unison recitation.

TAKING NOTES FROM AN ORAL PRESENTATION

Behavioral Objective. When given an oral presentation or thirty-minute duration, on any topic within the pupil's vocabulary knowledge, reasonably well organized, and developed at a normal pace, the pupil will be able to write appropriate notes in outlined form without any cues or prompts.

Entering Behavior. The pupil has adequate hearing, vision, and motor coordination. His "strategy" for note taking is to try to transcribe verbatim; he or she encounters difficulty trying to write and listen simultaneously.

Sequential Components

1. from outlining reading selection (and/or thoughts) to taking notes from speaker

2. from *brief* lecture (speaker stops) to longer

3. from having tape recorder (going back to verify) to no tape (*one* presentation only)

4. from supplying the pupil with an outline handout prior to the elector (requiring filling in) to no outline

5. from easier material to harder material

6. from personalized material to more general

7. from exaggeratedly *slow* presentation to faster

8. from perfectly organized talk to one including some tangentials

9. from having important (and difficult words) printed on the chalkboard to no such aid

10. from providing cues (e.g., "abbreviate," "write the numeral, not the word," "think of one-summary word" to no cues

11. from an oral abstract of the talk with discussion (pencils down) to taking notes

12. from a tutor (teacher, teacher aide, volunteer) taking notes part-time (alternating with pupil) to the pupil functioning independently

13. from a subject with which the pupil is familiar to new ones

Instructional Procedure

1. Begin with a brief reading selection (two paragraphs), below grade-level on a subject of personal interest. The pupil is handed an outline (requiring fill-ins). Provide verbal cues—"abbreviate," etc., a tutor alternates with the pupil in completing the fill-ins.

2. Same as step 1, but gradually increased to a selection on grade-level or three to four pages in length.

3. Same as step 2, but introduce more general subjects.

4. Same as step 3, but eliminate the outline handout.

5. Same as step 4, but fade out the assistance of tutor.

6. Same as step 5, but fade out verbal cues.

7. Repeat steps 1–6 while taking notes an a brief oral lecture (instead of from a reading selection). The presentation is perfectly organized, spoken exaggeratedly slowly, and the pupil is provided a tape recorder for verification.

8. Same as step 7, but speak in normal tempo.

9. Same as 8, but gradually increase the length of the presentation of the full thirty minutes.

10. Same as 9, but start interjecting some portions containing tangential points.

11. Same as 10, but gradually eliminate the use of the tape recorder.

Effective Teachers

Once the goals and objectives are set, instruction follows. Regardless of the population or subject area effective teachers generally (Lochner and McNamara, 1989):

- plan for small increments of change
- use modeling, prompting, and shaping
- provide for practice, review, and generalization
- provide feedback and reinforcement
- evaluation instruction

In addition to these generic competencies, effective teachers recognize that, regardless of the presence or absence of a disability, students learn in different ways. They are aware that if all students' needs are to be met, then they must modify their presentation:

1. change how instruction is delivered
2. change the student response
3. change who delivers instruction
4. change the condition of instruction

Let me elaborate on each of these modifications.

1. *Change how instruction is delivered.* Rather than the typical verbal-lecture-discussion model, you may want to use various *media presentation,* such as filmstrips, slides, tape recordings, overhead transparencies, opaque projectors, and the like. Teaching machines, such the "Language Master," "Little Professor," "Speak and Spell" all employ specific instructional programs for academic skill acquisition.

Teachers should also consider the use of *learning centers* throughout the classroom. This can be used as a primary means of instruction or supplementary. Good learning centers consist of clearly stated objectives, specific directions, samples of the work to be completed, a schedule for students, and a record-keeping procedure.

Programmed instruction is another alternative to the typical teacher-student interaction. Programmed materials provide small, repetitive instruction to students. Usually, the student is provided with immediate feedback, thereby reducing failure.

Many students with learning/behavioral problems learn best through what has been called "experimental learning," that is, they learn best by

doing. Use of concrete materials, "real life" experiences, role playing, simulations, and problem-solving are examples of methods of changing the manner in which instruction is being delivered.

Finally, providing the student with a *parallel alternative curriculum.* This
allows the student who is functioning below grade-level in reading, for example, to acquire the same material in the content area as his/her peers. You
can have the tests put on audio tape, you can reduce the complexity of the
book by adapting it (this is very time consuming!), you can locate books
covering the same content written on a lower level (see publisher of your
current text), or you can use oral presentation instead of written material,
such a film and filmstrips, as well as the audio tape previously mentioned.

2. Change the student response.

- tape answers

- dictate answers

- type answers

- do projects

- use graph paper to align work

- provide cues for recall

- use consistent format

3. *Change the conditions of instruction.* teachers do not have to be the
only ones who provide instruction in the classroom. Students can—and do—
learn from each other. Peer tutoring and teaching devices can be employed
in such a way that students have an opportunity to learn from others. These
can be coupled with the techniques listed above and should be taught of as
a viable option in all classrooms.

4. *Change the conditions of instruction.* Students teachers may want to
vary the classroom or organization so that some instruction can be in a large
group, some a small group, some peer tutoring, etc. The "where" of instructions is also important for any students. Therefore, you can try to provide
work space for students in specific areas of the room or on the perimeter of
the group. Some students need study carrels to avoid distraction, while others
find such work places too confining. Others effective alternatives for presenting information to students are:

- Use advance organizers

- provide background information

- motivate students to learn

- point out the advance organizer to learn
- identify topics and tasks
- provide a structured framework for the class period
- clarify required activity
- introduce vocabulary
- state concepts to be learned
- state expected outcome
- Provide a list of sample *PRIOR* to reading assignments of lectures
- Provide written back-up to oral directions and lectures
- Allow good note takers to use carbon paper to make copies of their notes for problem learners
- To maintain attention:
  — combine visual/auditory presentations
  — establish eye-contact with students during oral directions/lectures
  — write assignments/objectives on board
  — pause every six to eight minutes during a lecture for question
  — give examples and demonstrations
  — review throughout
  — summarize at the end of each lesson
  — give cues concerning what is important

These general competencies set the framework for specific remedial techniques, which are discussed below.

Remediation of Specific Disabilities

The plan of intervention must be derived from a thorough assessment of the student. However, for the learning disabled student who is educated in a multicultural, multiethnic urban environment, this is not often the case. Attention to the concerns addressed within this text and a shift from current assessment procedures is necessary. Once that occurs the appropriate practices discussed below can be implemented.

Reading Instruction

There will always be considerable debate over the most effective reading method (Smith, 1995). Teachers of learning disabled students must be aware of the most frequently employed methods and typical problems encountered by them described by Smith (1995, pp. 436, 437, 438). The six approaches are presented below. Included are the cautions that should be exercised when working with learning disabled students. These cautions are particularly important for a culturally and linguistically diverse population in that they may not possess the experiential and linguistic background necessary to succeed. Moreover, the teacher must be aware of the cultural and sociolinguistic background of their students in order to select the reading approach that is most appropriate.

APPROACHES TO READING INSTRUCTION
AND
CAUTIONS WITH RESPECT TO LEARNING DISABLED STUDENTS

1. Visual Approaches
Visual methods are often referred to as "look-say" because words are taught by visual discrimination of letters and remembering what several letters grouped together look like. The contours of the words are highlighted in order to help children distinguish and remember them:

CORN   POND   KITE

Many basal readers (grade series developed for the average reader) incorporate a visual approach in beginning reading (e.g., Scott Foresman).

Eventually decoding skills are added. Comprehension is emphasized throughout.

Caution
The visual approach encourages the poor reader's impulsive "look guess" strategies. Most children will deduce phonetic rules when they have learned enough words, but poor readers won't.

2. The Phonics Approach
The phonics method teaches children to associate printed letters with their corresponding sounds. Children can then use these phonic skills to analyze sound sequences, blend them together, and pronounce new words. "Pond" will be sounded out (pu-ah-nn-di) and then blended together again. A variety of reading series emphasize the phonic method (e.g., Engleman and Carnine's" (1976) Distar program emphasizing phonics skills are a useful adjunct to any program (e.g., Spalings, *The Phonovisual Method;* Schoolfield and Timberlake, 1960).

Caution

The phonic method will be difficult for the child who has trouble discriminating among sounds and initial and terminal letter sounds, blending sounds into words, or remembering the sounds of letters and words.

Phonics will be difficult for the one who takes so long to retrieve one sound that the previous ones are forgotten.

3. The Linguistic Approach

Linguistic theorists emphasize the strong relationship between printed words and reader's oral language skills. Since meaning precedes the printed word, and individual sounds don't occur in oral language (there is no real word such as "pu-ah-nn-di"), the linguistic method tries to shortcut combining letters to yield words, so that the reader can concentrate on meaning. Once the student has learned to decode, reading for meaning can take place (Glass, 1973).

In a way, the linguistic approach combines visual and phonic methods. Word stems like *at* and *ick* are taught as sight words and then individual sounds are substituted at the beginning of the stem: *pat, rat, cat; pick, kick, sick*. Stems are taught that can be placed at the beginning (e.g., *un, dis*), end, or middle of words. There is definite sequence to the presentation of words, regular spelling patterns first, followed by irregular forms.

Caution

Some programs assume that the reader will be able to independently discover the relationship between the sound and the letter; this link may be difficult for the disabled reader.

Although this system has the advantages of using visual analysis while reducing the phonetic load, students may still be overloaded by having to learn too many sounds at once.

4. Languages Experience Methods

The language experience method emphasizes comprehension because the child's language is the foundation upon which reading skills are built. The child uses personal vocabulary to orally relate personal experiences. The teacher writes these on wall charts. If the child can answer meaningful questions about the story, he or she is directed to look at the individual words and letters, and try to remember them. Activities such as illustrating, editing, and making permanent charts or books are encouraged. This approach encourages creativity, motivation for learning to read, and aids speaking, listening, spelling, and writing skills.

Caution

Though capitalizing on visual processing, motivation, and reading for meaning, it is unlikely that learning disabled students will discover sound-symbol relationships for themselves.

The variety of words that need to be read and remembered may be confusing.

5. Personalized Reading Approach

The personalized reading approach has been adopted by many alternative schools that wish children to read what is most meaningful to them. The goal is to erase the stigma of being behind everyone else that comes from being assigned to the "Blue Bird" graded reading group instead of the "Hawks." It represents a much broader way of thinking about reading than other approaches.

The student chooses material that is of personal interest (books, magazines, newspapers) and reads at his or her own rate. It is highly motivating for students to participate in this type of independent approach.

Caution

Teachers must engage in systematic and continuous review because the learning disabled reader may be "getting in over his head." It is highly motivating for students to share in this approach.

6. Whole Language Approach

A whole language approach seeks to immerse students in a supportive, stimulating, natural learning environment that promotes their literacy. In a whole language approach, reading, writing, listening, speaking, and thinking are integrated as part of each lesson and activity.

In a whole language approach, the emphasis is on reading for meaning rather than learning decoding skills in isolation. Students are motivated to read and improve their reading by reading real, relevant, and functional materials. Thus, the whole language classroom is stocked with books of varying degrees of difficulty and content such as novels, short stories, dictionaries, and encyclopedias.

Caution

Due to the increased popularity of this approach, there is a great deal of misunderstanding reading a whole language philosophy, and therefore, misapplication of the principles that underlie whole language.

7. Programmed Instruction

Programmed instruction materials are the most extreme behaviorally oriented materials. They allow the student to be actively involved in learning and to progress at his or her own rate. The teacher is merely a guide. Programmed materials are presented in small sequential steps. The reader gets immediate feedback about whether or not the answers are correct, and then engages in additional examples of those skills in which he or she needs further practice.

Caution

The lack of presentation of material in small steps and constant review may compound the learning disabled child's learning difficulties and reinforce learning of errors.

LD students usually need active teacher guidance and feedback; they cannot take independent initiative for learning, self-pacing, and self-correcting.

LD students usually need teacher checks on learning; they may be using the solving independently.

General Guidelines for Reading Instruction

1. Spend time reading. Too often disabled readers avoid reading. Increased time spent of literacy-based activities will yield positive results.

2. Read aloud to your students. This provides them with a good reading model and also develops a fund of information.

3. Provide a wide variety of language-based activities to enhance a student's experiential background and then level of comfort with the language of reading.

Written Language

Smith (1995) notes that written language causes the greatest difficulties for learning disabled students. This statement can be amplified for a culturally and linguistically diverse population. The emphasis here would be placed on communication through the written word. Handwriting becomes a concern when it interferes with legibility.

The goals of an effective program should be based on the following principles and conditions (Graham and Miller, 1980):

1. Handwriting instruction is direct and not incidental.

2. Because disabled students exhibit a diverse range of handwriting achievement, instruction is individualized.

3. The handwriting program is planned, monitored, and modified on the basis of assessment information.

4. Successful teaching and remediation depend upon the flexible use of a wide variety of techniques and methods.

5. Handwriting is taught in short daily learning periods during which desirable habits are established.

6. Skills in handwriting are learned in isolation and then applied in meaningful context assignments.

7. Teachers stress the importance of handwriting and do not accept, condone, or encourage slovenly work.

8. Effective handwriting instruction is dependent upon the attitudes of both student and teacher.

9. The instructional atmosphere is pleasant, and motivation is promoted through incentives, reinforcement, success, and enthusiasm.

10. Teachers practice lessons prior to presentation and are able to write a "model" hand.

11. Students are encouraged to evaluate their own handwriting and, when appropriate, actively participate in initiating, conducting, and evaluating the remedial program.

Considerable time should be spent on written language. Following the hierarchy of learning presented herein, written language will be affected when oral language and reading are impaired. Too often it is assumed that it will automatically occur. Research does not suggest such a notion. Further, very specific instruction must be employed. Isaacason (1988) posits four general principles of effective writing instruction. They are:

1. Allow sufficient time for writing instruction

2. Teach writing as a process

3. Teach writing through interactive group experiences

4. Avoid excessive use of corrective feedback

Isaacson (1988) elaborates on each principle (pp.31, 32):

1. *Allow sufficient time for writing instruction and practice.* Research on effective teaching practices has pointed out the importance of instruction time and on-task practice time in increasing student achievement (Wilson and Wesson, 1986). Graves (1985) stated that children need to practice writing a minimum of 4 days each week to see any appreciable change of their writing.

2. *Teach writing as a process.* Skilled writers spend time considering what will be written, sometimes making notes or drawing diagrams. They keep their communication goals in mind as they transcribe those thoughts into writing. They periodically review and revise their compositions, making changes in content as well as correcting spelling and grammatical errors. Since most basal language arts textbooks do not teach writing as a process

and often overlook reviewing and revising stages almost entirely (Harrington-Borgan, 1983), teachers must plan their own instruction, emphasizing the entire process from planning to revision. Process instruction can be supplemented with activities such as sentence combining, vocabulary substitution, or punctuation exercises that are effective in developing specific skills.

3. *Teach writing through interactive group experiences.* Hillocks (1984) found that the most effective approaches to writing instruction are those that maintain high levels of student interaction in structured problem-solving tasks. Group brainstorming activities are an effective way to generate enthusiasm for the citing task (Crelock, Hutchinson, Sitko, and Marlett, 1985). The teacher then can model planning skills by helping students to organize their ideas or information in a diagram, grid, or activity. First-draft compositions can be read in small groups to give the authors feedback for revision.

4. *Avoid excessive use of corrective feedback.* Teachers must be sensitive to the negative attitudes that mildly disabled students bring to the act of writing. Keeping a student's instructional objective clearly in mind enables the teacher to provide corrective feedback only for aspects of composition that have been taught and related to the objective. Considering that learning correct spelling, punctuation, and grammar takes many years, teachers should restrain from circling or red-penciling mechanical errors every time they appear.

The focus must always remain on written expression. This is also the case with spelling. Spelling must be integrated into the entire language arts program; it cannot be taught in isolation. The more interrelated the instruction, the higher probability is that students will transfer skills across the curriculum (McNamara, 1989). A survey of practices in spelling revealed a number of methods deemed to be effective, and an equal number deemed to be ineffective (Vallecorsa, Zigman, and Henderson, 1985).

Survey of Practices in Spelling

Effective Methods	Ineffective Methods
Using a test-study-test procedure.	Using a test-study approach.
Initially testing a few words daily	Presenting words in sentences or paragraphs.
Using high-interest activities and motivational games.	Having students write words in the air to aid retention.
Emphasizing a core of high-frequency words list.	Relying on commercial materials as foundation of the spelling program.
Teaching words that are part of generalizations and student's listening and speaking vocabulary.	Emphasizing spelling rules.

Effective Methods	Ineffective Methods
Teaching strategies for whole word study.	Permitting students to devise their own methods for studying spelling words.
Having students correct their own spelling work under the teacher's direction.	Using a synthetic alphabet.
Using a variety of remedial techniques rather than one approach.	Limited phonics instruction in teaching spelling.
Developing students' dictionary skills.	Developing students' proofreading skills.
Frequently reevaluating words studied.	Presenting words in a list initially. Having students write words several times to aid retention.

(Vallecorsa, Zigman, and Henderson, 1985)

Mathematics

Math instruction must begin with concrete manipulative material. This material should relate to the experiences of the student. Too often, the example, the word problem, and the pictures presented verbally and in mathematics textbooks are not relevant or interesting to the students. Teachers should employ a wide variety of materials (newspapers, magazines, pictures) and examples that reflect the population they are teaching. Once students master skills at the concrete level, they are able to move on to paper and pencil tasks. Without such instruction they will fail. It is important to reduce the complexity of the task and increase the student's attention to detail. As a number of texts note (Siegal and Gold, 1982; McNamara, 1989; Smith, 1995), the teacher must use a great deal of ingenuity and creativity in math instruction because there is a dearth of curricular materials geared toward the learning disabled student. Siegal and Gold (1982, pp. 242–44) provide a number of interventions for common math problems encountered by learning disabled students.

1. *Guessing answers, impulsive responses.* Prevent impulsive responses rather than the number of items completed. Do not present many examples of problems at one time. Some children respond to "so much work" by racing through, trying to get it over quickly. For these children, withhold their pencil, while they think through the problem. For oral responses, encourage "thinking time," rather than speed of response.

2. *Difficulty in completing work.* Many workbooks have too much material in them, causing distraction. For this child, too, fewer items should be

presented at one time. A cardboard window can be used to frame each example or problem while blocking out others on the page. Behavior modification techniques can also be helpful.

3. *Repetition in writing numbers.* Some children tend to perseverate and continue writing a response beyond what is appropriate. This happens frequently when drilling in writing numbers. Structure the assignment or page so that repetition will not be encouraged. Do not have the child write the numeral more than once before introducing another numeral.

4. *Repeating a computational operation.* To prevent continuation of operations, alternate operations are required so that a pattern is not established. In some cases it may be necessary to alternate modes of responses of materials.

5. *Auditory memory deficits.* Visual presentations can be linked with the auditory, so that the child is not limited by the weaker modality. The visual representation can be stressed.

6. *Visual memory problems.* Children who have difficulty revisualizing numbers can learn to use verbal prompts or mediators. Some respond best if a motor cue is taught. Color cuing can sometimes be utilized. Process signs can be written in different colors. Problems can be given orally.

7. *Dysgraphia.* When children have difficulty in writing numerals, alternatives must be considered. Writing should be kept on a minimum. Printed or duplicated materials can be used so that only answers need be filled in. In some cases, the child can be directed to underline the correct response from among three or four. A stamp pad and numeral stamps can be provided so that the child need only stamp in the correct answer. Answers can be given orally to the teacher or aide, or on a tape recorder.

8. *Erasing difficulties.* This is a problem, though minor, which can adversely affect children's written performance. Frequently they do such a poor job that they cannot separate what was rewritten from what was erased. Another factor should also be considered. Some children are fearful of making errors. By teaching them how to erase an error, we are also saying that mistakes can undone.

9. *Difficulties distinguishing size, shapes, length, and/or amounts.* Provide a variety of real materials for comparison to arrange in order of size, length, weight, and so on. All senses should be utilized: touching, looking, counting aloud. Such activities can be done simultaneously with some children, but with a single sensory approach with others. Stern blocks and pattern boards or Cuisinaire rods can be used to build trains and stairs so the children can compare size, length, and numerical combinations.

Concept words such as "heavy-light," "bigger-smaller" must be taught using cut-out dolls, photos, and so forth. Ask questions such as: "Which clothes will fit which doll?" "Which car is the right size for the garage?" Children also need experiences in weighing and measuring items. The child should initially learn to feel the difference between one pound and five pounds; then finer discriminations should be learned.

Puzzles and form boards provide clues to shapes. Discuss the shape needed to fill the space. Have the child feel and describe the shapes without looking at them. Many learning disabled children have verbal strengths and these should be tapped in various learning situations (Johnson and Myklebust, 1967, p. 254). Large outlines of shapes can be placed on the floor. The children can trace the shapes placed on the floor. They can trace the shapes as they walk along the edges.

10. *Deficits in estimating time or chronological sequence.* Have the child estimate how long he or she thinks an activity will take. Have them show on a demonstration clock what it will look like when the time will be up. Compare the time on the demonstration clock with the actual time.

Using a timer, have the child attempt to complete a task before it rings. The teacher should integrate the use of time concepts in natural classroom situations: e.g., "we have five minutes to learn before it is time to go to lunch."

To facilitate memory of sequence steps, verbal or visual cues can be used. Charts can show step-by-step procedures. Verbalizations should be clear and concise. This skill is important in learning to follow directions in a recipe but also in performing computations and in doing two-step and three-step problems.

11. *Difficulties in maintaining columns.* Writing numerals in columns can be aided by providing a strong visual and possible tactile stimulus. The space for writing the examples can be set off by a heavy line or a raised barrier (cardboard frame). Colored lines on the paper can set off the place-value columns. Using ruled paper with the lines running vertically can also provide the needed structure. As proficiency is developed, the stimulus should be faded.

12. *Orientation problems.* The concepts right-left, up-down, in-out, under-over, and so on, should be used in real situations in the classroom and them applied to workbook or other two-dimensional planes. Because of the concrete thinking of many learning disabled children, they have difficulty transferring concepts understood in the "real world" to the two-dimensional world of their texts and workbooks. Specific teaching of the relationship between the real and representational frequently has to be provided. Cues such as a color or shape may be used to show directions. Arrows can be used to indicate the direction in which to work calculations.

Learning How to Learn

Providing culturally and linguistically diverse learning disabled students with basic skill instruction is critical, but not sufficient. Students need to go beyond this level an acquire competencies in the acquisition, storage, and recall of information. Collier (1988) notes that students from culturally and linguistically diverse backgrounds have even more difficulty with this type of strategic learning than other learning disabled students. One approach, learning strategies, developed at the University of Kansas Institute for Research in Learning Disabilities (KU-IRLD) (Deshler, Ellis, and Lenz, 1995), teaches students "how to learn." Their curriculum has three major strands: (1) strategies that assist students in acquiring information for written materials; (2) strategies that enable students to identify and store important; (3) strategies for facilitating written expression and demonstration of competence. Some of the major instructional principles are listed below (Deshler and Schumacher, 1986).

1. *Match instruction with curriculum demands.* The first step in this process is to understand exactly what types of curriculum demands the student is failing to meet (not taking, test taking, and so forth). This is a change of focus from assessment of student deficits to assessment of environmental demands. Academic programs are then developed to provide those strategies that will enable the student to succeed.

2. *Use structured teaching methodology.* The methodology employed in the learning strategy approach is as follows: (1) the student is assessed to determine his/her current learning habits regarding a particular task; (2) a new strategy is described to the student (component steps, rationale, results the student can expect, and situations when it can be used); (3) the new strategy is modeled for the student; (4) the student used verbal rehearsal; (5) the student practices with material closely approximating that used in the regular classroom; and (7) the student performs the strategy in the regular setting and is involved in evaluating.

3. *Deliberately promote generalization.* The researchers at KU-IRLD believe, as does Anderson-Inman (1986), that the "acid test" of instruction is the degree to which the skills are generalized across settings and maintained over time. This is accomplished by (1) making students aware of the contexts in which the strategy can be applied; (2) providing ample opportunity for practicing strategies in a wide variety of settings as with a variety of materials; and (3) providing for communication between regular and special educators.

4. *Apply "critical teaching" behavior.* These teaching behaviors are as follows:

a. Provide appropriate positive and corrective feedback

b. Use organizers throughout instruction

c. Ensure high levels of academic response

d. Provide for youth involvement in discussions

e. Provide regular reviews of key instructional points and checks of comprehension

f. Monitor student performance

g. Require mastery learning

h. Communicate high expectations to students

i. Communicate rationale for instructional activities

j. Facilitate independence

5. *Use scope and sequence in teaching.* This is more of a plea than a guiding principle. It suggests that teachers need to plan a program over years if students are to become competent in a large number of strategies.

6. *Ensure that teaching decisions are governed by outcome goals.* Students must become aware of how they learn and of realization that they have control over their own learning. By monitoring their progress in systematic fashion and evaluating programs by outcomes, the teacher can greatly facilitate this process.

7. *Maximize student involvement.* Simply stated, students must feel a sense of ownership in their academic program.

8. *Maintain realistic point of view.* The authors point out that not all students will benefit from this approach. Wise practitioners are aware that not all school failure can be attributed to a lack of appropriate learning strategies.

When employing such strategies with a more diverse learning disabled population, the teacher must address five major areas: (1) cultural and linguistic background; (2) experiential background; (3) acculturation level; (4) sociolinguistic development, and (5) cognitive learning styles. Hoover and Collier (1992) believe these areas have a great deal of importance in the instruction of learning strategies. They are summarized:

1. *Cultural and linguistic background.* This refers to the cultural context or situation within which one is most familiar as well as the associated language. Cultural/linguistic background has a comprehensive effect on how

and why knowledge skills are acquired. Problems may arise if this background is different from what is expected in the educational setting (Collier, 1988).

2. *Experiential background.* Differences in experiential background affect minority students' responses to different aspects of curriculum. As a result, the types of strategies and skills used to learn are highly dependent upon prior experiences. Methods used to acquire study skills and learning strategies are also influenced by experimental background.

3. *Acculturation level.* Acculturation is the process of adapting to new cultural environments. It frequently involves integrating new cultural patterns into one's existing cultural framework. Adequate acculturation is essential for learning to occur. A minority student's level of acculturation heavily influences academic and school performance (Cummins, 1984; Juffer, 1983).

4. *Sociolinguistic development.* This refers to a student's language acquisition and development. In particular, one's Basic Interpersonal Communication Skills (BICS) and Cognitive Language Proficiency (CALP) must be determined. BICS represents the more "surface" language skills, while CALP reflects "deep" language structure and development. CALP must be developed to adequately deal with academic work (Cummins, 1984).

5. *Cognitive learning styles.* Cognitive learning styles reflect characteristic ways in which students respond to learning tasks and instructional environments. Much research has been conducted in this area, and although results are inconclusive, knowledge of one's cognitive styles may assist in understanding a student's preference toward learning (Good and Brophy, 1990; Woolfolk, 1990). When used in conjunction with the other four areas, cognitive style preferences may assist in the appropriate selection and use of various study skills and learning strategies for minority students with learning disabilities. Additionally these authors selected six learning strategies and ten study skills that are of particular importance to this population (pp. 229–31).

Learning Strategies and Special Considerations

Active processing. Effective in developing CALP. Students may experience difficulty using this strategy if they lack necessary concepts due to experiential background or cultural differences. Cross-cultural assistance may help students to activate prior knowledge and elaborate on learning new skills or concepts.

Analogy. Previously acquired experiences in one's cultural/linguistic and experiential background are emphasized through this strategy. Familiarizing oneself with the students' culture and language background will increase staff sensitivity as students attempt to understand new concepts of skills by drawing analogies to their existing language and cultural knowledge.

Copping. This strategy assists students in dealing with academic as well as nonacademic situations. May help to build self-esteem, lower anxiety levels, reduce confusion in control, and address other aspects associated with the process of acculturation.

Evaluation. Diverse students often require the use of visual cues as well as verbal descriptions to successfully use this strategy. Sociolinguistic development and acculturation levels will affect the success of this strategy and influence the amount of visual/verbal cues required. Greater levels of CALP also reflect success levels with this strategy.

Organization. Cognitive styles of learning, experiential background, and cultural/linguistic background all influence the manner in which students organize or cluster items, tasks, or responsibilities. Sensitivity to the student's culture and language background will help alleviate problems between student and teacher preferences toward organization and grouping tasks.

Rehearsal. Students experiencing problems with acculturation who have limited experiential background may find this strategy useful as they confront new and more difficult tasks or situations. Rehearsal procedures can be described bilingually to ensure that the student fully grasps the process in a way meaningful to his or her cultural/linguistic background.

Study Skills

Reading rate. Sociolinguistic development is important to consider when assisting students to select and use various reading rates. In addition, one's cognitive learning style preferences may facilitate greater use of specific reading rates. Cultural background may influence a perceived purpose, which may be different from an instructor's purpose.

Listening. It is essential to determine that students comprehend as well as gear verbal messages. CALP levels, cultural background, and learning styles influence listening abilities. Some cultures may favor more nonverbal versus verbal interactions.

Note taking and outlining. Using culturally relevant cues is essential to helping students with diverse cultural experiences take effective notes.

Sociolinguistic development levels will influence the complexity levels students can successfully address when note taking or outlining.

Report writing. The complex task of writing is directly affected by language proficiency. Content in written reports should reflect cultural background and experiences. Understanding a student's CALP, preferred learning styles, and cultural influences are essential for assisting in writing.

Oral presentation. Acculturation levels and sociolinguistic development influence a student's oral presentation skill development. Poorly acculturated students may experience great difficulty with this skill.

Graphic aids. Unfamiliarity with visual material may be a direct result of a diverse cultural background. Poor development of CALP may reflect insufficient language necessary to adequately comprehend the meaning and relevance of visual material in the broader context.

Test taking. Individual performance on tests may not be a primary concern of students from various cultures. Rather, group achievement may be of greater importance than individual performance. This, along with acculturation levels or language proficiency, will influence one's test-taking abilities.

Library usage. A student's learning style, experiential background, and culture will influence his or her proficiency in using a library. Poorly acculturated students may need step-by-step cues and instructions concerning the proper use of a library.

Reference material. The extent to which a student is knowledgeable of various reference materials will vary based on language development and cultural experiences. As with library usage, culturally diverse students may require specific cues, including culturally appropriate examples, in use of different reference materials.

Time management. Managing time may be very difficult for some students who come from cultures where time is viewed in less static ways. Students with less acculturation abilities or inconsistent learning styles will find time management difficult.

Cooperative Learning

Much has been written regarding the implementation of cooperative learning for a linguistically and culturally diverse population (see Slavin, 1983; Johnson and Johnson, 1994, for detailed discussion). Cooperative learning appears to be particularly useful for diverse groups of students in that it encourages groups of students to work together. Lyman, Foyle, and Azwell (1993) provide a summary of cooperative learning strategies.

STAD (Slavin 1983) is one of the easier strategies to use because subject content can be presented in the traditional way. Individual student assessment can use the teacher's traditional criteria and methods. After the teacher presents the lesson, student teams work on assignments cooperatively in order to master the subject's material. In studies conducted by Newmann and Thompson (1978), STAD was the most successful of the cooperative learning techniques studied when compared with traditional teaching methods.

TGT (Slavin 1991) is similar to STAD but with the addition of a competitive tournament. After studying the material with team members, students compete with other students of similar achievement levels to win points for their teams. Individual student assessment is then conducted.

Jigsaw II (Slavin 1991) places students in groups to read parts of a chapter, article, or text, or to read different materials dealing with a similar topic. The students meet to review their readings. Then student groups are reformed so that original team members are divided among "expert" groups with other students from other teams who have read the same material. After discussion within the "expert" group, students return to their original teams to further discuss the material. Questions about the material can be provided to the original teams or the "expert" groups. Assessment of learning is done by test or quiz on an individual basis to insure individual accountability.

Learning together is a strategy promoted by Johnson and Johnson (1991). Students are given cooperative tasks that are intended to create positive interdependence and encourage group interaction. Rewards may be provided for both individual and group performance.

Group Investigation (Sharan and Sharan 1992) requires that students work together to decide what information is needed how the information will be organized and presented. In organizing the tasks and facilitating group work, teachers encourage students to develop the skills of applying information, synthesizing information, and inferring from information related to the subject being studied.

Spencer Kagan (1990) has developed and promoted a wide rage of simple cooperative learning structures. One such simple structure in *Roundtable*. It can be used for group building, reviewing information, practicing skills, and brainstorming. Students are grouped in heterogeneous teams of three or four. Each team has a single sheet of paper and one pencil or pen. The teacher asks a question that has many possible correct answers. Each student contributes one possible correct answer and passes the paper clockwise to another student in the group. After time is called, teams with the most correct answers are recognized. Each team then discusses its work and identifies possible ways to improve. A variation has each student in the team start a piece of paper by writing an answer and passing it on so that several papers are circulating at the same time.

Frank Lyman (1993) of the University of Maryland has developed *Think-Pair-Share* (TPS). TPS can improve student participation and interest in class discussions. Because the strategy is easily implemented, it provides a successful first experience in cooperative learning for elementary school students. In TPS, students listen while the teacher poses a question or problem related to the learning objective. The students try to come up with possible answers individually. After students have had the opportunity to consider the question or problem individually, they are paired with another student to discuss or work on their responses. The teacher obtains responses from the paired discussion groups. TPS allows each student to become actively involved in learning by sharing ideas with at least one other student. TPS is supported by research on wait-time and cuing.

Prior to implementing cooperative learning, you should consider the following guidelines suggested by Lyman et al. (1993):

1. *Start slowly.* Use cooperative learning sparingly until you are sure that what you are doing is benefiting the class.

2. *Avoid group grading.* Group grading can alarm parents of high achievers. Group grading is only for skilled practitioners of cooperative learning, and then only when adequate parent and administrator information have been provided in advance.

3. *Build an atmosphere that encourages cooperative learning.* Building student ownership, active participation, high expectations, and positive feelings create a foundation for cooperative learning and for successful classroom management.

4. *Promote student success.* Early experiences with cooperative learning should be highly successful and rewarding for students.

5. *Tell administrators you are using cooperative learning methods.* Be ready to explain your goals, expected outcomes, and the benefits to research associates.

6. *Use other techniques and strategies as well as cooperative learning.* No technique is effective when used all the time.

7. *Monitor student reactions and conduct individual conferences with students.* This helps reassure those who are troubled by cooperative learning.

8. *Teach group processes to students.* Don't expect your students to already have the skills needed to work successfully in groups.

9. *Monitor the effectiveness of your teaching.* Use the same individual evaluation procedures you usually use. You may also wish to monitor student achievement; attitude; attendance; discipline referrals; and behavior in the playground, hallway, and lunchroom as indicators of the success of your methods.

10. *Network with other teachers.* A support group of other teachers who use cooperative learning is necessary for problem solving, celebration, and exchange of ideas (pp. 29–30).

5

Classroom Management

This text does not advocate a particular classroom management approach for a specific group of children—"classroom management techniques for Asian-American students" or "classroom management techniques for Native-Americans," etc. Rather I believe it is critical to understanding the needs of the students being taught. That understanding includes knowledge of the cultural and linguistic background of students as well as their interests, concerns, and aspirations. Individuals within any ethnic group may vary considerably depending upon their specific experiences.

Teachers should be aware of the characteristics of the students in their class. Davidman and Davidman (1994) developed the profile below. It accomplishes the following:

1. Introduces you to the ethnic, cultural, and instructional diversity that exists in the classroom.

2. Provides you with instructionally relevant information about specific special learners who are included in the data base.

3. Shares with you new categories of students that the district currently finds useful for instructional or funding reasons.

The Classroom Demographic Profile

Student
Teacher
Name: _____

Cooperating
Teacher
Name: _____   Date: _____

Grade: _____   School: _____   District: _____

The Classroom Demographic Profile *(continued)*

Types of Students   Instructionally Relevant
[Students are or have an (n)]   Information about Specific Students

A. Linguistically Different (LEP/NEP)
(first name only)

1. _____

2. _____

3. _____

B. Individual Education Plan (IEP/LEP)

1. _____

2. _____

3. _____

C. Suspected Learning Disability but No IEP/LEP

1. _____

2. _____

3. _____

D. Of Ethic Minority Background**
(first name and ethnic identification)

1. _____

2. _____

3. _____

4. _____

5. _____

6. _____

7. _____

8. _____

9. _____

10. _____

The Classroom Demographic Profile *(continued)*

E. Migrant Students

1. _____

2. _____

3. _____

4. _____

F. Receiving Special Medication

1. _____

2. _____

3. _____

G. Gifted and Talented

1. _____

2. _____

3. _____

H. Other Categories Used by Classroom Teachers and/or School

_____

_____

_____

_____

I. Extra Spaces

_____

_____

_____

_____

_____

**Include here students of Hispanic-American, African-American, Native-American, Asian-American, Iranian-American, and Punjabi-American background only if this classroom teacher believes the student's cultural background or ethnicity has, or might have, instructional implications (pp. 62, 63).

All teachers must be effective managers of classroom behavior. This is probably more true for teachers in urban areas where the resources are diminishing and the class size is large. Reynolds and Birch (1977) note that the inappropriate behaviors exhibited by special education in the regular classroom present greater problems for the teacher than do academic deficiencies. The effective teacher provides a positive, reinforcing environment (Albert and Troutman, 1995). Being aware of the cultural and sociolinguistic background of students will enhance the classroom atmosphere. However, regardless of the population taught, the dignity of each student is to be respected. This section will be subdivided into three sections dealing with (1) minor disturbances (2) moderate inappropriate behaviors, and (3) severe behavior problems.

Minor Disturbances

One approach that has been effective in dealing with such problems has been dubbed "Super School." During the 1971–1972 and 1972–1973 academic years a demonstration classroom was established by the University of Kansas and the Lawrence (Kansas) Unified School District No. 497 for the purpose of applying behavioral management procedures in a regular classroom (Hopkins and Conrad, 1976). The first year of the project focused on the third grade, and the second year focused on the third and fourth grades. The classes were heterogeneously grouped and included special education students who attended the resource room. Some of the teaching methods employed were as follows:

1. *Praising students who were working.* The teacher verbally praised all students who were on task. Initially her rate was between five and ten per minute. Once appropriate behavior patterns were established, this practice gradually faded.

2. *Descriptive praise.* A specific description of the behavior being reinforced helped the students understand why they were being reinforced, and it also served to cue other children. For example, " I like the way Mary is in her seat; she'll be able to complete her assignment."

3. *Praise across the room.* The procedure enabled the teacher to deliver reinforcement to a large number of students. Obviously she could not see their work, but she could reinforce appropriate on-task behavior.

4. *Nonverbal reinforcement.* In addition to verbal praise, many students respond to smiles, winks, pats on the back, hugs, and other types of nonver-

bal reinforcement. This approach also allows the teacher to deliver higher rates of approval.

5. *Privileges.* These were only given contingent upon appropriate behaviors. Too often students are given privileges for inappropriate behaviors, such as the student who is the monitor because he or she has engaged in inappropriate behavior and the teacher wants to "keep him or her busy." Inadvertently the teacher is reinforcing negative behaviors.

6. *Positive comments on paper.* All papers received some special comment regardless of the accuracy of the assignment. The teacher could comment on the effort expended, even if that effort did not produce the desirable results.

7. *Ignoring inappropriate behavior.* Because of the high rates of reinforcement, the teacher was able to ignore inappropriate behavior, and the greater majority of them were extinguished.

8. *A simple punishment procedure.* All classroom rules were clearly listed of the board. If a student broke these rules, a point was placed on the board. The student lost five minutes of recess time for each point. It is important to note that this approach was only used as a last resort. If a student received a large number of points, the teacher would check herself or himself to see that students were being reinforced at appropriate levels.

The results of this project bought about a remarkable gain in academic and social behaviors. Often regular educators remark that the process of mainstreaming takes time away from nondisabled students. This project, as well as other research (Kazdin, 1973; Drabman and Lahey, 1974) indicates that there are vicarious effects of reinforcement. In "Super School," for example, the disabled students displayed marked improvement, and it was even greater for their nondisabled peers.

Another set of procedures was discussed by McDaniel (1986). He notes that these procedures represent an eclectic point of view and have been demonstrated to be effective. They are as follows:

1. *The focusing principle.* Essentially, this basic principle suggest that the teacher should get the student's attention *prior to* giving instructions or presenting material. It lets the student know that the teacher believes what he or she says is important.

2. *The principle of direct instruction.* This refers to getting the students on task quickly and keeping them engaged in on-task behavior. Having a contract

for the day or a file or folder that they can consult will alert them to their responsibilities and will prevent unnecessary interruptions.

3. *The monitoring principle.* Here McDaniel suggests frequent movement about the room to allow the teacher to evaluate student progress and performance. The teacher can provide feedback, prevent the student from "practicing failure," and refocus the student.

4. *The modeling principle.* Teachers must provide their students with food models of appropriate school behavior. Teachers should be prompt, organized, and well mannered, and should exhibit self-control so students will have a role model to emulate. At all costs, they should avoid sarcastic remarks and speak in a soft, low-pitched voice.

5. *The cuing principle.* McDaniels believes that good teachers have always used cues to improve discipline. Raising a hand for silence, pointing to classroom rules, and employing a sign that says "work zone" can all help to remind students of the task at hand. The use of cues can be very helpful and allows the teacher to use his or her creativity in developing novel cues.

6. *The principle of environmental control.* One thing a teacher can exercise a great deal of control over is the classroom environment. A teacher can add or take away stimulating activities depending upon their effects on student behavior. This control can also be accomplished through teacher behavior, which can alternately stimulate or calm students in the class.

7. *The principle of low-profile intervention.* Management in the classroom should be as discreet, unobtrusive, and smooth as possible. Confrontations and public encounters should be avoided. Teachers must be aware of the need to anticipate behavioral difficulties and develop a systematic plan of interaction. This is much more effective than rapidly escalating a minor problem.

8. *The principle of assertive discipline.* This combination of reinforcement and limit setting has been set forth by Canter and calls for a higher-profile type of intervention. The assertive teacher clearly states the expectations for student behavior and develops positive and negative consequences for the class.

9. *The-I message principle.* Basically, I-messages can be employed in two ways: (1) by a specific request ("I want you to . . .") or (2) by communication of feeling ("when you do_____ I feel_____ and it angers me"). McDaniels believes that both can be employed as one of the many interventions. In a

teacher's repertoire, effective classroom management can eliminate most minor disturbances.

Moderate Inappropriate Behaviors

These are behaviors that require a more consistent, data-based approach in order to be substantially reduced or eliminated. In these cases the teacher must be skilled in identifying the behavior, in collecting and recording data, in using reinforcement and punishment techniques, and a token economy system.

Identifying Target Behaviors. The initial step in the development of a systematic intervention plan is the identification of a behavior in observable and measurable terms. Although this appears to be a reasonable and simple starting point, it often represents a major stumbling block for teachers, be they regular or special educators. It is common practice to assess academic problems through the use of objective instruments such as formal standardized test, informal criterion-referenced tests, and teacher-made tests. We engage in such practices because it is crucial to pinpoint the student's strengths and weaknesses, how they approach tasks, and how they respond to instruction in order to develop a remedial program that has high probability for success. However, teachers rarely apply such rigorous conditions to the assessment of behavior problems.

Teachers often discuss a student's behavior in vague and nebulous terms or focus on the possible reasons for this behavior. Such discussions may be helpful in understanding the nature of a child's difficulty, but they will rarely, if ever, enable the teacher to develop an intervention plan that can be carried out in the classroom. A behavioral approach demands precision, from the identification of the behavior to the evaluation of the effectiveness of the intervention plan. Therefore, the teacher must define exactly what behaviors are to be increased or decreased: for example, whether he or she wants to increase in-seat behavior, to decrease the number of times Joseph talks out, to increase raising hands to ask a question, to decrease the number of times John hits Louis, and so forth. All of these behaviors can be observed: that is, we can see if the behavior occurs—we don't have to infer. Moreover, they can be measured: we can count the frequency or duration of each. Most, if not all, classroom behaviors can be staged in observable and measurable terms.

Following is a list of behaviors typically emitted by students. Column A presents the problem in behavioral terms, and Column B clearly defines the target behavior:

Not Measurable	Measurable
1. Student never pays attention.	1. Increase the percentage of time the student spends on task (eye-contact with the teacher, looking at textbook, writing when appropriate).
2. Student is very hostile.	2. Decreases the number of times the student hits another student.
3. Student does not have any friends in class.	3. Increase the number of positive comments made to the target student by fellow classmates. Increase time spent with other students.
4. Student has a poor self-concept.	4. Increase the number of positive self-statements. Decrease negative comments regarding work of self.
5. Student is always interrupting.	5. Increase the number of times the students wait his or her turn to speak.
6. Student wanders around the room.	6. Increase in-seat behavior.
7. Student is never on time.	7. Increase on-time behavior during a specified period.
8. Student does not respect others' property.	8. Decrease the number of times the student defaces another student's work.
9. Student appears to have a great deal on his or her mind.	9. Decrease off-task behavior (looking out the window, lack of eye-contact, not following directions).
10. Student is a very aggressive child.	10. Decreases the number. of times the student pushes another student.

As can be seen from the above, refinement of the description of behaviors allows teachers to focus on a specific behavior, communicate more effectively with colleagues, administrators, and parents, and begin to collect data on the frequency and duration of behaviors emitted by students. The last mentioned, accurate recording-keeping, is one of the cornerstones of a behavioral approach to classroom management. Often teachers believe that the paperwork associated with this approach is overwhelming. However, upon close examination they realize that it can be a very effective use of time. Madsen and Madsen (1974) discuss a case in which a teacher refused to "waste time with all that book work" (p. 31). When observed by an independent observer, this teacher was recorded saying "Now stop that talking" more than one hundred times in one morning session. Obviously these negative comments took considerable time away from teaching, whereas the record-keeping procedures could be developed so that they would be less time-consuming and more productive than the repetition of negative instructions.

There are numerous recording methods available to teachers, but four appear to have the greatest applicability. They are (1) event recording, (2) duration recording, (3) time sample recording, and (4) direct measurement of permanent products.

Event Recording. This involves the collection of raw frequencies of behavior. It is used for discrete events, those typically lasting less than two minutes. Behaviors that lend themselves to this type of recording are the number of times a child is out of his or her seat, the number of times a student comes late to class, the number of times a student talks out in the classroom, and the number of times a student hits his or her classmates. Holms (1966) employed this type of recording to count the disruptive classroom behaviors of a nine-year-old boy. Physical aggression was the target behavior of a study undertaken by Brown and Elliot (1965), which also employed this method of collecting data.

Clearly, the teacher must be able to collect the data in a manner that does not interfere with the ability of the teacher to move about the room and provide instruction to students. The author has found a wrist golf-counter the best device for this purpose (see *Journal of Applied Analysis* (1968) *1*, 77–78). It allows the teacher movement and provides him or her with a readily available, inconspicuous data collection device. Other ways in which events can be recorded are by marking a piece of adhesive tape adhered to the wrist, moving small objects (paper, token, toothpicks, etc.) from one pocket to another, or using a small tally sheet or index card. Usually a thirty-minute observation period is adequate.

Duration Recording When behaviors occur for a long period of time, duration recording is the most appropriate procedure. Certain behaviors such as temper tantrums, leaving the classroom, and taking time off task, may not occur frequently but may occur for a relatively long period of time. When a behavior occurs for longer than two or three minutes, collecting data on the time elapsed may be more meaningful than recording procedure in the investigation. Madsen and Madsen (1974) recorded the percentage of time a seven-year-old girl was sucking her thumb and the percentage of time spent on the task was recorded by Ferritor et al. (1972). Although a stopwatch would be the most accurate way to collect this data, the minute hand on a wall clock or wristwatch can be used as long as the recorder can keep accurate record of time elapsed. The observation period is divided into equal intervals. If a student emits the target behavior at the end of the specified interval, it is recorded as a plus; if her or she does not emit the behavior, it is recorded as a minus. In the illustration below, a thirty-minute period is divided into ten three-minute intervals in order to record the percentage of time a student is in his or her seat. By the use of a stopwatch, wall clock, or wristwatch, the teacher observes the student at each three-minute segment. At the six-minute interval the student was out of the seat; therefore a minus was recorded. This process is continues until the thirty-minute period expires. The percentage of time spent in seat is obtained by dividing the number of intervals into the number of interval of in-seat behavior and converting this figure to a percentage. In this case the student was in his or her seat at 50 percent of the time.

In-Seat Behavior (30-minute intervals)

+	−	+	−	+	+	+	−	−	−
3	6	9	12	15	18	21	24	27	30

Although a thirty-minute interval is used most often, longer observation intervals may be necessary for specific types of behaviors.

Direct Measurement of Permanent Products. Although inappropriate behaviors are problems unto themselves, often they interfere with the acquisition of academic skills. To obtain data on this interference, the teacher can record data on a number of items, such as teacher-made tests, workbooks, pages completed, and the like. These data can be presented in raw frequency of percentages. Madsen and Forsythe (1974) used direct measurement of a permanent product to record the accuracy of the responses of sixth-grade students when they worked with an individual mathematics kit. In such cases teachers merely record the student's score on a daily basis. The tendency is to use this data collection procedure exclusively for academic behaviors that are caused by behavioral problems (such as off-task behavior) that should not be overlooked.

Charting Baseline Data. All the behavioral data can be displayed in a similar fashion on a graph. The ordinate (vertical axis) is labeled with a scale representing the behaviors emitted in terms of frequency or percentage, and the abscissa (horizontal axis) is labeled with the time dimensions, such as minutes, days, or observations (Hall, 1971; Alberto and Troutman, 1995). Teachers will want to collect and display data in such a way so that they will be able to evaluate the effectiveness of their intervention plan. Typically baseline data are collected for at least one week; then an intervention plan is implemented. A more detailed explanation of each of these stages follows.

If we are to make educational decisions based on factual information, not intuition or feelings, then we must add precision to our teaching. The first step is to establish the *baseline,* which can be defined as the operant level of behavior—that is, the level of behavior prior to intervention. Therefore, during the first five days of data collection, the student must be unaware of the procedure so that an accurate reading can be obtained. Typically, the baseline will last five days, but one must examine the data prior to moving on to the next stage. In baseline A (see next diagram) a desirable behavior, such as in-seat behavior, is increasing; therefore, one should simply continue taking baseline data. In baseline B, an undesirable behavior, such as yelling out, is decreasing by itself; therefore, one should not implement an intervention but should continue to observe the behavior and record baseline data. A stable baseline is illustrated in baseline C. It is going up and down but is within reasonable parameters; therefore, it is appropriate to intervene.

Next a plan must be developed and implemented that will either increase an appropriated behavior or decrease an inappropriate one. An example is presented on the following pages. The behavior is to increase as a result of the intervention on day six. The importance of charting behavior cannot be overemphasized. (See figures 5.1 and 5.2.) It is imperative if we are to add precision to our teaching in the special education or mainstreamed setting.

Reinforcement. Anything that increases in behavior is a reinforcer (McNamara and McNamara, 1995). The contingent use of reinforcement—that is, applying reinforcement after an appropriate behavior has been emitted—has brought about an increase in a wide variety of behaviors emitted by children and adolescents in educational settings. Hall et al. (1971) used contingent teacher attention and praise to decrease "talking out" in a special class setting. There has been consistent evidence that teacher attention (teacher proximity, verbal and nonverbal approvals) may act as an effective reinforcer for preschool and schoolage children (Harris et al., 1966; Hawkins et al., 1966; Thomas, Becker, Baer, and Baer, 1968; Madsen and Madsen, 1981). Bushell (1873) notes that "it has already been established that approval and

Figure 5.1 Three Types of Baselines

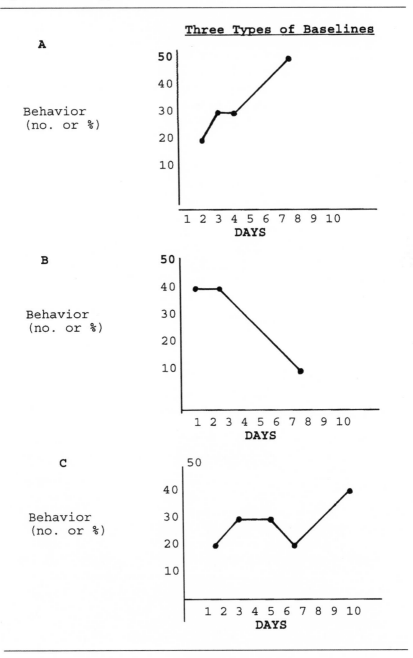

Figure 5.2 Three Types of Baselines

Student's Name

Behavior
(number or
  percent)

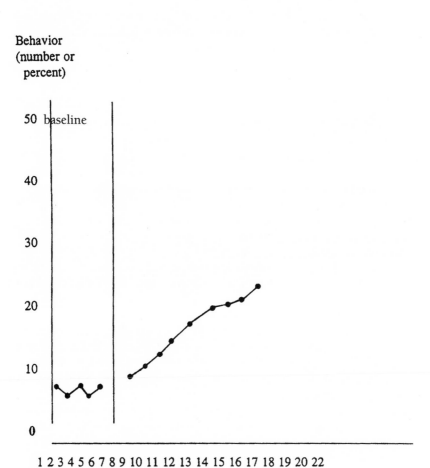

DAYS

praise of the teacher is an effective reinforcer for most children" (p.71). Teacher approval is perhaps the most easily accessible technique of reinforcement and should be used in special and regular classroom settings to increase appropriate student behavior.

Madsen and Madsen (1974) report that teachers who engaged in high approval rates have less behavior problems in the classroom. They conclude that this improvement in behavior is directly related to the amount of attention teachers give to appropriate student behavior. Therefore, reinforcing appropriate student behavior and (to a great extent) ignoring inappropriate behaviors, should be a management tool used by all teachers. Other reinforcers that can be employed in the mainstream setting are free time, privileges, stars, stickers, notes, positive notes, to parents, and the like. For a thorough list of reinforces available in most classrooms, see Madsen and Madsen (1974), pp. 182–92.

Punishment.   A punishment is anything that decreases the strength of a behavior (Hall, 1971). It is imperative that teachers be aware of the negative effects of punishment. O'Leary and O'Leary (1976) caution teachers to use this technique sparingly because students tend to associate the punisher with the punishment. This relationship will clearly interfere with the establishment of a good rapport between teacher and student. Hall (1971) has noted that one does not build up a repertoire of appropriate behaviors by employing punishment techniques; one simply eliminates the inappropriate behavior. Also to be considered is the effect of modeling this behavior for students who view the teacher as a standard for appropriate behavior. In most cases behaviors can be changed through the systematic application of reinforcement techniques. However, there may be times when a negative consequence is necessary to change a behavior.

Tate and Baroff (1966), Bucher and King (1971), Kiegal and Covert (1972), Hanser (1973), and O'Leary and O'Leary (1976) have used punishment techniques ranging from verbal reprimands to removal of privileges to reduce inappropriate student behaviors. Greer and Dorow (1976) note that punishment is not the first choice and that an approval rate of four to one is most desirable—that is, the teacher should be emitting at least four positive commands for every one negative comment. Investigations by Madsen and Madsen (1974), White (1975), and McNamara (1977) indicate that this is not the prevailing mode of teacher behavior.

Token Economies.   Token economies have been employed in various environments, including the classroom (Kazdin, 1973). Briefly, such as a system involves having students earn tokens (or points, stars, checks, etc.) contingent upon desired behaviors. At a later time, usually the end of the week, the student can exchange his or her tokens for prizes. These prizes may be edibles, toys, privileges in the classroom, or virtually anything available that can serve as a reinforcer. As Stephens and Cooper (1980) point out, tokens are not a cure all, nor are they ends in themselves. Hall (1971) notes that they should only be employed as a last resort, when other reinforces fail to bring about desired changes in behavior. Teachers must also realize that the record-keeping involved with tokens is extensive and may not be a cost-effective use of time. Other disadvantages, as well as advantages, of the token economy are listed by Stephens and Cooper (1980).

Contracting. If students are to succeed, there must be improved communication between regular and special educators regarding the students' homework contracts to reinforce appropriate behavior and improve academic and social behaviors. Homme (1970) describes the many uses of contracts in the classroom. They can be used for special subjects, academic subjects, homework assignments, or other similar areas of schoolwork that need specific attention. An example of a homework contract is presented below. The teacher and the student jointly decide on the number of assignments that must be completed as to the reward that will be given.

Sample Homework Contract

Student's Name _____

Homework

Subject	Mon	Tues	Wed	Thurs	Fri
Reading					
Math					
Spelling Hand Writing					

I will complete _____ homework assignments.

My reward will be _____

Teacher _____ Date _____
           (signature)

Student _____ Date _____
           (signature)

Structured Learning.   Goldstein et al. (1980) have developed a program to teach adolescents appropriate prosocial behaviors. They employ a structured learning approach that incorporates examples of competent skill behavior, opportunities to rehearse, systematic feedback, and transfer of skill to real life settings. They have identified fifty structured learning skills, which are presented below. Teachers can select those skills that are appropriate for their students with moderate inappropriate behaviors and can follow the specific guidelines described by Goldstein and his colleagues (1980, pp. 84,85).

Group I—Beginning Social Skills

1. Listening
2. Starting a Conversation
3. Having a Conversation
4. Asking a Question
5. Saying Thank You
6. Introducing Yourself
7. Introducing Other People
8. Giving a Compliment

Group II—Advanced Social Skills

9. Asking for Help
10. Joining In
11. Giving Instructions
12. Following Instructions
13. Apologizing
14. Convincing Others

Group III—Skills for Dealing with Feelings

15. Knowing Your Feelings
16. Expressing Your Feelings
17. Understanding the Feelings of Others
18. Dealing with Someone Else's Anger
19. Expressing Affection
20. Dealing with Fear
21. Rewarding Yourself

Group IV—Skill Alternatives to Aggression

22. Asking Permission
23. Sharing Something
24. Helping Others
25. Negotiating

26. Using Self-Control
27. Standing Up for Your Rights
28. Responding to Teasing
29. Avoiding Trouble with Others
30. Keeping Out of Fights

Group V—Skills for Dealing with Stress
31. Making a Complaint
32. Answering a Complaint
33. Showing Sportsmanship after the Game
34. Dealing with Embarrassment
35. Dealing with Being Left Out
36. Standing Up for a Friend
37. Responding to Persuasion
38. Responding to Failure
39. Dealing with Contradictory Messages
40. Dealing with Accusation
41. Getting Ready for a Difficult Conversation
42. Dealing with Group Pressure

Group VI—Planning Skills
43. Deciding on Something to Do
44. Deciding What Caused a Problem
45. Setting a Goal
46. Deciding on Your Abilities
47. Gathering Information
48. Arranging Problems by Appointments
49. Making a Decision
50. Concentrating on a Task

Severe Behavior Problems

There are students who consistently display severely inappropriate behaviors and appear to lack an understanding of appropriate rules for conducting oneself in school. For these students it may be necessary to teach social skills directly. Initially, the teacher must assess those skills that need to be taught. Typically these social skills can be identified in terms of problem behaviors. Cartledge and Milburn (1980) list the following problem behaviors and accompanying social skills to be taught:

Problem Behaviors	Social Skills
1. The child calls another uncomplimentary names.	1. The child makes positive remarks to others.
2. The child frequently interrupts.	2. The child waits for pauses.
3. The child makes negative statements about his or her ability.	3. The child identifies something he or she does well.
4. The child cheats when playing with peers.	4. The child plays games according to the rules.
5. The child throws tantrums when teased by ignoring.	5. The child responds to peer teasing.
6. The child laughs at or ignores individuals in need of help.	6. The child assists individuals in need of help.

Teachers may identify target social skills for individual students, as well as for groups. The teaching process can be broken into five steps: (1) providing instruction (2) exposure to a model, (3) rehearsal, (4) performance feedback, and (5) practice.

Providing Instructions. Students with learning or behavioral problems require direct instruction for those skills that capable learners appear to acquire incidentally. Most certainly this is the case with social skills. The teacher must provide explicit instructions about the skills to be taught. This can be done through the use of specific objectives from the student's IEP or by generating lists of expected behaviors for a wide variety of social skills. For example, Silverman, Zigmond, and Sanzone (1981) have identified a group of skills subsumed under the head *teaching-pleasing behaviors*. Anyone who has worked in special education is well aware of the problems the students have when interacting with regular classroom teachers. It is often observed that these students do not know how to "get along" with these teachers. Using the five-stage process developed by Cartledge and Milburn (1980) and the content from the teacher pleasing behavior parts of the School Survival Skills Problem (Silverman, Zigmond, and Sanzone, 1981), the resource room teacher would begin by providing instructions. For example, students must realize that certain behaviors are expected in each classroom. At times these rules will be explicit, and at other times they must be inferred. Perhaps the simplest approach would be to briefly discuss what is expected in general, such as by saying "All students are expected to be in class on time," or "All students must bring a pen and paper to class," or "All students are expected to raise their hand before talking." The teacher must provide the students with sufficient information to enable them to understand what is expected of them.

Often students act in an inappropriate fashion because it was assumed that they knew how to behave. This approach makes no such assumption; it provides the student with the instructions necessary to comprehend what the expected behavior is prior to engaging in a violation of a social skill.

Exposure to a Model. Instructions alone will be insufficient to bring about an increase in social skills. Students must have an opportunity to observe individuals who model the appropriate behavior. This can be done in a number of ways—through the use of role playing, pictorial representations, films, slides, books, and the like. Ample exposure to appropriate models will enable students to see how the social skills can be manifested in a wide variety of settings and under different conditions.

Rehearsals. Students should be encouraged to think about the setting in which the social skill is to demonstrated and to practice the skill. Some students find the use of visual imagery very helpful. They try to imagine the situation in the classroom and "see" themselves carrying out the appropriate social skill successfully. Role playing is also helpful when rehearsing a social skill. Students can try the social skill as other students play the role of the teacher and other students.

Performance Feedback. During the rehearsal of social skills the teacher must evaluate the student's performance. Although these activities are enjoyable in and of themselves, the goal is to increase the student's ability to increase their social skills. Therefore, feedback must be given to enable them to redefine their understanding of the procedure. The feedback should be immediate and overwhelmingly positive: that is, the same principles of reinforcement discussed previously apply here. Students should be provided with frequent positive feedback regarding their performance. At times, neutral comments may need to be made about a specific skill, but all efforts must be made to ensure that students do not receive punitive rewards regarding their ability to rehearse the social skill.

Practice. When the social skill has been demonstrated in the special education setting, the student is ready to generalize the skill. It is obvious that this is the goal of social skill training; it is not sufficient to display these behaviors in isolation. Ample opportunity must be give for practicing the skill, and reinforcement must be given contingent upon performing the skill in training.

Cartledge, Lee, and Feng (1995) believe that cultural patterns impact the social skills performed in the classroom. They feel it is critical to understand cultural distinctions in order to develop appropriate social skill instruction.

They provide information regarding the four largest minority cultural groups in the United States: Hispanic Americans, African-Americans, Native Americans, and Asian Americans. The cultural distinctions they note are listed below (pp. 329–30, 334–35, 341–43, 346–48).

Hispanic Americans

Although Hispanics are not a singular group, there are some prevalent features of the culture worth noting that potentially impact social behaviors observed in the classroom:

1. Strong gender roles are defined. The concept of maleness, or machismo, is related to courage, superiority, and sexual prowess. The ideal man is one who never breaks down or cracks (Maldonado and Cross, 1979). As a husband, the man is an authoritarian, the head and master of the household.

2. Family unity is one of the most sacred values. The unit is an extended family, with relatives interacting daily as friends, consultants, and financial and moral supporters.

3. It is considered shameful to deal with the law. The concept of "the law" includes legal services and government agencies.

4. Children are desired but are taught to give unquestioning obedience and respect to their parents and authority figures (Wells, 1990).

5. Interpersonal, affective, or emotional relationships are cherished. The orientation is expressive.

6. Passivity and deference to others are encouraged as the ultimate in civilized behavior, as opposed to the aggressiveness reflected in the larger society. Children are discouraged from fighting, even in self-defense (Henderson, 1979).

7. While interpersonal relationships are cherished, the integrity of the individual is not to be violated with group pressure. Ghali (1979) speaks of the fear of relinquishing one's individuality in order to conform, and Henderson (1979) notes the difficulty of accepting the concept of teamwork.

8. Members are protective of their Hispanic culture and are reluctant to adopt "American" lifestyles.

9. The culture is bilingual. Spanish is spoken fluently in the home. The primary language is characterized as earthy, direct, and unadorned with metaphors. Accented English is the second language for many.

10. There is an orientation toward satisfying current need and enjoying life in the present. A zest for life has been noted by various researches (Litsinger, 1973; Henderson, 1979; Lewis, 1979).

11. There is a fatalistic acceptance of destiny or life as it exists.

12. Hispanic Americans do not identify themselves with any specific racial background because they are a composite of many races and civilizations. Their Spanish, black, and Native American heritage is reflected in all ranges of skin colors, hair textures, and features. For many, color becomes an issue for the first time when they arrive in the United States, when they are judged to be either black or white. Problems of identity within families often start when some members are considered white while others are regarded as black.

13. Nearly one third of all Hispanic Americans live below the poverty level. The rate of unemployment is significantly higher than the national average (the Commission on Minority Participation in Education and American life, 1988).

14. Hispanic Americans have the greatest proportion of high school dropouts (Wells, 1990).

Educators must be sensitive to the fact that some instruction delivered in school may contradict what children learn at home (teaching them to be assertive, to be critical thinkers, or to question authority). Students can become aware of new alternatives without the teacher minimizing or undermining the children's respect and affection for their parents' instructions.

African-Americans

1. The role of the church has been influencial in the lives of the people. Largely Protestant, African-Americans have been observed to attend church in greater proportions and with greater regularity than other groups.

2. Group members are noted to be xenophilous—comfortable with strangers—as opposed to xenophobic (fearful of outsiders).

3. Although comfortable when associating with different people, there is a reluctance to reveal personal information freely.

4. Music plays a functional role—as a means of communicating with God, for courtship, and for comfort. Black culture brings to mind spirituals, gospel, blues, jazz, soul music, and rap.

5. The black family traditionally has been an extended family "stretched horizontally in every direction as well as vertically. . . taking into account all members of the community" (Goode, 1979). The orientation is a sense of oneness with the community, and toward the survival of its members.

6. Emphasis is placed on respecting one's elders. Older generations orally relate the history of the family, serve as baby-sitters for working parents, and volunteer the wisdom that comes with their years.

7. Children are encouraged to be "tough" to survive and overcome disparities in the real world. They may be conditioned not to unquestioningly trust all authority figures.

8. A sense of pride in self is encouraged. Educational and occupational milestones are greeted with special recognition and celebration.

9. Time is thought of in two dimensions—past and present. Potential time, or future time, is considered "no time." Henderson (1979) classifies the experience of blacks and time as an "African survival": time begins when an event is performed. This is in contrast to setting a specific time prior to the occurrence of an event.

10. The group is monolingual. Nevertheless, members understand a variety of usages for a single word or phrase, and some communicate in a special dialect that is different from mainstream English. Parallel to communicating with words, African-Americans closely observe gestures, intonations, and facial expressions.

11. Life expectancy is less than that for other cultural groups, and mortality rate among infants is higher and rising.

12. Academic achievements are below the levels of the majority-group peers, and students are disproportionately represented in special education classes (as are Hispanic Americans). Nationally, African-American children represent 17 percent of all students, but constitute 41 percent of the special education population. Of the African-American special education population, 85 percent are males (Kunjufu, 1989).

13. Cognitive styles vary, but many students are reported to achieve maximally when instruction is interactive and "hands-on," as opposed to passive, or in the hear-write channel exclusively.

14. Childrearing practices of most families would be labeled as "controlling" (or "authoritarian") as opposed to "democratic." In the controlling orientation, parents tend to stress obedience, respect, neatness, cleanliness,

and staying out of trouble. They are more likely to use physical punishment, and are sometimes arbitrary in their discipline. This practice may have resulted from three centuries of slavery where physical aggression was modeled as a principal means of control and compliance. According to Maccoby (1980), this style seems to be more damaging to boys than girls, based on research showing boys in these families display more dependent, angry, and defiant behaviors. A similar effect in boys appears to result from permissive parenting.

Native Americans

Cultural Distinctions

Trying to make generalizations about all Native American nations would simply perpetuate stereotypes, while overlooking intra- and intertribe diversity. Another limitation of current research is the lack of long-term, in-depth qualitative studies that investigate multiple dimensions of a group people. A presentation of various tendencies related to social skills will be qualities whenever possible by identifying specific tribes associated with the social behavior. Patterns of social behavior that have emerged are not only tribe-specific, but may be age- and gender-specific as well.

Nature of Interactions

Play Behaviors. Young Native Americans of various nations are described as socially active. Little boys and girls, ages two through seven, play together freely with enthusiasm under the watchful care of an older sister. Clear lines are then drawn between the genders around age eight (Navajo, Hopi). Vogt, Jordan, and Tharp (1987) found that the formation of same-gender dyads and triads was a culturally appropriate classroom adaptation that enhanced the effectiveness of motivation management. This kind of separation of genders persists throughout life.

Games are spontaneous and creative. Children are prevented from hurting themselves but otherwise are not restricted from teasing, tagging, and so on. They are observed interacting with a Caucasian first-grade male in a successful study (Bergsgaard and Larsson, 1984).

When many Native Americans reach age ten, however, they are expected to distinguish themselves physically and behaviorally from younger children. Young men do not play with little boys, and it is at this time that they would be expected not to engage in any one-on-one physical confrontations as younger children do. It is not manly to do so (Hopi). A spirit of cooperation and harmony with peers and others is strongly valued and reinforced not only for the Hopi, but for the Navajo, Creek, and Choctaws as well (Vogt et al., 1987; Scruggs and Mastropieri, 1985; Greenbaum, 1985). Greenbaum (1985), using video cameras to record data in four fifth- and sixth-grade classrooms in Mississippi, notes that Choctaws would not compete against peers for grades or criticize classmates.

Close Friends. It is worth noting that for many Native-American children, the closest friends typically are not found and made in the classroom. Best friends very frequently are close relatives (Schneider, 1993). Alexander (1991) lived across the street from a child her age and attended public school classrooms in Tulsa. Yet her "best friend who was like a sister" was a first cousin who lived twenty miles away. The two families got together at least once a week, and she recalls those visits as "special times" with partings that were difficult. For the Creek and others (e.g., Hopi), a value stressed from the early years is to know who your larger family is and respect its members (Alexander, 1991; Saslow and Harrover, 1968; Henderson, 1979).

Verbal Behavior. For the very young, many accounts report that singing, talking, and role playing, in concert with traditional parenting practices, are uncensored. Various researches report older children's "reticence" or unresponsiveness in the classroom (e.g., Mahan and Criger, 1977; Schneider, 1993; Youngman and Sadongie, 1974). Hopi children, and those of many other nations, are inclined to be silent in class. They may be labeled shy or uncommunicative: teachers report that questions directed to a Native American individual consistently may not be responded to, even though the student knows the answer.

In stark contrast, Choctaws speak out in the classrooms setting. Compared to their Anglo counterparts, Choctaw students interrupt the teacher more often and must be taught the skill of alternating listening with speaking. Greenbaum (1985) refers to the need to teach them "switchboard participation." Although they speak out at will, it has been noted that Choctaw students use shorter utterances and gaze at their peers while the teacher is talking more than do students from the majority culture.

Various patterns of verbal behavior emerge not only by tribe but by gender within tribes. Alexander (1991) asserts that Creek women, for instance, are considered aggressive speakers, and that this characteristic "should not be viewed as an anomaly."

Prosocial Behavior. Demonstrations of anger or aggression are the exception rather than the rule for Native Americans. Navajos are reported to value a sense of humor, laughing often and not taking themselves too seriously. In the culture, young men and women are trained to be good-natured in interactions with each other. This absence of aggression may be attributed partly to "the spirit of belonging" considered characteristic of Native American societies (Brendtro, Brokenleg, and Van Brockern, 1990, p. 37). Children are reared in communities where they are nurtured, taught, and supported by all members. Accordingly, they are helped to acquire a sense of belonging to all other individuals as well as to nature, which, in turn, encourages them to live in harmony with others and their physical surroundings.

Traditional Native American practices have undergone some marked changes in recent decades. Brendro et al. (1990), note historical attributes of the culture, including (1) a sense of belonging, (2) a spirit of mastery, (3) a spirit of independence, and (4) a spirit of generosity. From early childhood native-American children were encouraged to strive toward mastery in every human domain: physical, cognitive, spiritual, and social. Instructions came through stories that taught ways of behaving, games that encouraged competence and group participation, and work that fostered responsibility. In their quest for mastery, children were motivated to achieve personal goals, not to be superior to others. More skilled individuals were not viewed as competitors, but as models who were establishing a standard to be attained.

The development of independence and autonomy were extremely important features of the child rearing practices within Native American cultures. Although children were encouraged to make independent decisions, it was hoped that, through instructions and modeling, children would respect their elders and acquire a set of behaviors consistent with their community. Emphasis was placed on being self-disciplined rather than obedient, promoted largely through "kindly lecturing" rather than punishment.

Generosity of altruism completed this Native American circle of life. Acts of selfishness were frowned on. Although property was held privately, favor and prestige were extended to those who gave generously rather than to those who accumulated massive holding.

Hall (1993) describes the National Indian Youth Leadership Project (NIYLP), which builds on the Native American heritage and promotes a concept of "servant leadership":

> The model of a servant leader has been passed down in the ancient languages of our people. It is available to a world too often broken by selfishness, exploitation, and domination. The lesson we must teach our young is simply stated in these old Navajo words, IAA goober': "Having compassion for others above all" (p. 29).

At the seventh and eighth grade, youth attend a multicultural leadership camp to acquire skills and experiences they are to apply when they return to their respective communities. Training sessions vary, ranging from whitewater rafting to a leadership seminar. An understanding grows that true leadership results from helping and empowering others. Sample community projects that have emerged from such training include adopting kindergarten students for reading and tutoring services, and painting murals on the walls of a senior center. Reported effects on the Native American youth include increases in self-esteem and the development of higher-level thinking, problem-solving, and conflict-resolution skills.

Asian Americans

Cultural Distinctions

The same reservations apply here as with the preceding culturally diverse groups. Asian Americans certainly are not a monolith, and there are sufficient inter- and intragroup differences to warrant extreme caution in discussing cultural commonalities. Nevertheless, there are some frequently occurring patterns that impact the child's social development and need to be addressed in the context of social skills instruction for Asian American students. Based on the literature describing Asian and Western (U.S.) cultures, the two can be compared.

A major distinguishing feature of Asian societies is the central focus on the family and the greater emphasis placed on the family than on the individual. In Asian cultures, the family bond is systematically strengthened over one's lifetime, exercising considerable control over the individual's relationships and social behaviors. The reverse is more likely to be the case in the U.S. mainstream culture. Asian cultures tend to socialize their children to subjugate themselves to the will of the family, to be compliant, and to avoid any actions that would bring shame or disgrace to the family.

The U.S. population has more commonalities than differences. "The effective teacher acknowledges the distinctions of a cultural minority, but sees individuals as foremost" (p. 352).

Conflict Resolution

Johnson and Johnson (1996) developed the *Teaching Students to be Peacemakers Program* to teach students how to resolve conflicts. It has six steps:

1. *Create a cooperative context.* Considerable evidence and practical experience demonstrate that when individuals are in competition, they will

strive for a "win" in conflicts and not try to solve the problem. A problem-solving approach requires the disputants to recognize their long-term inter-dependence and the need to maintain effective working relationships with each other-conditions that exist only in a cooperative context.

2. *Teach students to recognize when a conflict is and is not occurring.* Many students see conflicts as always involving anger, hostility, and violence. They do not recognize conflicts as such when they lead to laughter, insight, learning, and problem solving.

3. *Teach students a concrete and specific procedure for negotiating agreements.* Everyone involved can thus achieve their goals while maintaining or even improving the quality of their relationship. Telling students to "be nice" or "talk it out," or "solve your problem" is not enough.

4. *Teach students to use a concrete and specific mediation procedure.* Give them enough practice in using this procedure to develop some expertise. If students are to mediate their schoolmates' conflicts, they must know how to do so. This initial training in the nature of conflict and how to negotiate and mediate usually consists of approximately thirty half-hour lessons.

5. *Implement the peer mediation program.* Working in pairs at first, the mediator's role is rotated so each student is mediator.

6. *Continue the training in negotiating and mediation procedures weekly throughout first through twelfth grades* to refine and upgrade students' skills. To become competent in resolving conflicts takes years and years. Any thought that a few hours of training is enough to ensure constructive conflict management is terribly misguided.

The research on the effectiveness of the program has been very positive. The authors believe that conflicts can be constructive and valuable.
To summarize:

- Conflicts can increase achievement and long-term retention of academic material.

- Conflicts are the key to using higher level cognitive and moral reasoning and healthy cognitive, social, and psychological development.

- Conflicts focus attention on problems that have to be solved and energize us to solve them.

- Conflicts clarify who you are, what your values are, what you care about and are committed to, and how you may need to change.

- Conflicts help you understand who the other person is and what his or her values are.

- Conflicts strengthen relationships by increasing your confidence that the two of you can resolve your disagreements, and by keeping the relationship clear of irritations and resentments so that positive feelings can be experienced fully.

- Conflicts can release anger, anxiety, insecurity, and sadness that, if kept inside, make us mentally sick.

- Conflicts can be fun. What determines whether conflicts result in these positive outcomes is how skillfully students (and faculty) use the integrative negotiation and mediation procedures.

6

Implications for Teacher Training

If the needs of linguistically and culturally diverse students with learning disabilities are to be met teacher training institutions and schools must provide appropriate programs. In this section, the major components of a teacher training program (preservice) and a professional development program (also referred to as in-service) will be discussed.

Preservice Teacher Training

Issues related to linguistic and cultural diversity and their impact on the assessment and teaching of urban children need to be addressed throughout the curriculum, not presented as an isolated issue. Special educators must develop a sensitivity to these issues as they relate to educational assessment, curriculum planning, and teacher-parent instructions.

Cultural diversity is an aspect of teacher training alarmingly absent in most training programs. Warren (1987) reported teachers themselves were well aware of the need for an incorporation of issues of cultural diversity into their training program. In a survey of how one hundred special education teachers in New York City assessed their preparation for teaching handicapped children, Warren found that "nearly one-third (31 percent) of the respondents felt inadequately prepared to adapt curriculum to work with students with limited English proficiency, while 58.4 percent of the teachers felt inadequately prepared to interpret the standard assessment measures that were appropriate for use with language-minority children" (p. 68).

When training programs for educators to address issues in "cultural sensitivity," they rarely acknowledge the complexities of either the culture concept or the cultures of specific social groups. Emphasis is usually placed of defining "what each group is like" in terms of "traditions" and "customs." Important variabilities *within* particular groups are ignored, with the danger that individuals will be stereotyped once identified as "belonging" to a specific category: "Hispanic," "black," "Asian," and so forth. In addition, relationships between various social groups and U.S. society are also ignored.

One basic principle of the training program is that trainees must be provided with a comprehensive understanding of minority groups that goes beyond traditional training programs in techniques and methodologies to incorporate knowledge of the sociohistoric contexts in which particular minority groups have developed. This entails not only the study of particular groups, but also developing a thorough understanding of the theoretical concept—"culture," "ethnicity," "minority," "social structure," etc.—necessary to understand particular groups as urban minority groups in the United States.

A second principle is that developing this comprehensive understanding must involve a variety of learning experiences, including opportunities to absorb information through lectures, reading, and discussion, through practice in conducting research projects, and through practical experience in applying this knowledge in practical settings. Programs must provide students with the opportunity to view cultural diversity and particular minority groups from a variety of perspectives, including that of the student, the researcher, and the practitioner.

New Forms of Assessment

Although a national interest has developed in educational reform including new forms of performance-based assessments, little documentation has been conducted on the factors that facilitate or impede assessment reform within a school (Falk, NCREST). Furthermore, preliminary school-based research studies have suggested that staff development is a critical component to the success of the reform effort. Teachers must provide their students with models of appropriate school behavior. Teachers should be prompt, organized, and well mannered, and should exhibit self-control so students will have a role model to emulate. At all costs, they should avoid sarcastic remarks and speak in a soft, low-pitched voice.

During the past few years a number of assessment reform projects have been supported by enthusiastic teachers and administrators who are actively engaged in educational restructuring and who are eager to effect real assessment reform. However, too many alternative, authentic or performance-based assessment projects have reached a plateau at the development of innovative and engaging activities, which are then presented as innovative and engaging assessment instruments.

An aggressive effort is also needed to effect systematic assessment reform in the nation's graduate teacher training programs in order to rethink the ways in which new forms of assessments are presented in training programs. Such an effort could bring about greater articulation between what teachers learn in their graduate classes and "the reality" of their classrooms.

Competencies

Below are the cultural diversity competencies critical for special education professionals. They should be incorporated into the special education curriculum:

A. Knowledge of the culture concept, including:

   1. different models of culture

   2. the relevance and implications of those models for understanding cultural diversity in U.S. urban settings

   3. the relationship of culture to social organization, economic and political spheres, institutions

   4. the cultural aspects of child development

   5. the relevance of culture concept to education

B. Understanding of ethnicity concept:

   1. different models of ethnicity

   2. interaction of ethnicity with culture, social, and economic conditions, politics

   3. history of specific ethnic groups

C. Understanding of specific minority groups, especially those in the U.S. urban settings:

   1. attitudes toward education, disability, U.S. society and institutions, and the like

   2. knowledge of U.S. institutions, schooling, service agencies, labor markets, and the like

3. participation in U.S. social institutions, political process, labor markets, and the like

4. communication styles, social networking

D. Understanding of cross-cultural communication issues in modern urban and institutional settings

E. Ability to establish professional relations with specific minority groups as teacher, assessment specialists, administrators

F. Skill in observation, interviewing, date collection, and the like

G. Skill in analyzing cultural data and applying it to professional practice

Educators serving ethnic minority populations need to be more than technicians applying assessment instruments, teaching strategies, or curriculum programs. They need considerable flexibility, a solid understanding of ethnic and cultural differences, and well-developed observational and analytical skills in order to provide assessments, educational programming, and related services that are appropriate to the needs and abilities of each minority child. This cultural sensitivity must be founded in a solid understanding of the particular minority groups being served.

Additionally, they need to be provided with the following experiences:

- Engaging teachers in self-awareness activities to explore their attitudes and perceptions concerning their cultural group and beliefs, as well as the effects of their attitudes on students in terms of self-concept, academic abilities, educational opportunities.

- Exposing teachers to accurate information about various cultural ethnic groups (for example, historical and contemporary contributions and lifestyles, value, systems, interpersonal communication patterns, learning styles, and parental attitudes about education and disabilities).

- Helping educators to explore the diversity that exists between, as well as within, cultural ethnic groups.

- Showing teachers how to apply and incorporate multicultural perspectives into the teaching-learning process to maximize the academic, cognitive, personal, and social development of learners (assessment, curriculum, and instructional management, strategies, and materials).

- Demonstrating effective interactions among teachers, students, and family members.

- Providing special education teachers with opportunities to manifest appropriate applications of cultural information to create a healthy learning climate (Ford, 1992, p.100).

The proposed training program is designed to provide the intellectual foundations and hands-on practical experience that educators need to best serve those ethnic minority populations most commonly encountered in the urban setting.

Grossman (1992) also provides competencies based on a thirteen-year project at the bilingual/multicultural special education program, San Jose State University. They are:

Bilingual/Multicultural Competencies

In addition to the competencies required for the regular special education credential, trainees also demonstrate additional competencies for working with Chinese, Filipino, Spanish, or Vietnamese-speaking LEP students with learning handicaps. The specific competencies required for the certificate of competency in bilingual/cross-cultural special education are as described below.

The selection of these competencies was originally based on the following:

• Deliberations of project directors and faculty members of IHE bilingual special education personnel preparation programs during the 1980 and 1981 national task oriented seminars sponsored by the U.S. Office of Education.

• Deliberations of the program advisory board, which was composed of representatives from LEAs and the SEA as well as the faculty of various departments of SJSU.

• The then current published expert opinion and reseach.

Since then, the program has been refined regularly on the basis of recommendations from LEA and SEA staff and program graduates, the results of internal and external evaluations, and new developments and insights derived from the practical experience and research of others. While the program faculty reads all the relevant research, they have been especially influenced by the publications of the following experts in the area of preparing personnel to serve culturally and linguistically different students with disabilities: Leonard Baca, Patricia Cegelka, Philip Chinn, Nancy Cloud, James Cummins, Richard Figueroa, Sandra Fradd, Herbert Grossman, Wayne Holtzman, Patricia Landurand, Alba Ortiz, Maximo Plata, Alphonso Preito, Robert Rueda, and James Yates.

The program contents are designed to impart the same competencies to all trainees in the Chinese, Filipino, Spanish, and Vietnamese language emphases, but the different competencies receive varying degrees of stress in each emphasis. Three examples of these program adaptations follow:

1. Almost all the trainees in the Chinese, Filipino, and Vietnamese emphasis are native speakers, many are not. All emphasis programs include courses taught in the target languages as well as in English. However, because there is a much greater need to improve the non-English language skills of trainees in the Hispanic emphasis, they take more of their course work in their target language.

2. Many more trainees in the Hispanic emphasis than in the Chinese, Filipino, and Vietnamese emphasis have already received training in bilingual education when they enter the program. As a result, fewer trainees in the Hispanic emphasis are required to enroll in EDSE 290B, the course that deals with bilingual and ESL methodologies.

3. The vast majority of LEP students with disabilities in California are Spanish-speaking. Trainees in the Hispanic program can realistically expect to work in special education settings in which all their students will be LEP Spanish speakers. This is not the case for trainees in the Chinese, Filipino, and Vietnamese emphasis. In addition, there is more assessment and instructional material available in Spanish than Chinese, Filipino, and Vietnamese. Therefore, less emphasis is placed in the Hispanic program on such competencies as working with interpreters and developing and adapting assessment and instructional materials in students' native languages.

The description below, therefore, is a generic description of all emphasis programs. In actual practices, there are differences between the programs like those described and explained above. The following are the additional bilingual/multicultural competencies included in the program and the activities followed to enable trainees to attain these competencies. The bilingual faculty routinely includes these competencies and activities in the courses they teach. The regular special education faculty usually do so since the competencies were infused into their courses as part of the multicultural grant. However, the extent to which they follow the "game plane" varies from person to person.

Language Fluency

1. The trainees are able to communicate effectively in Chinese, Filipino, Spanish, or Vietnamese with LEP students and their parents. (Admission to this program is open to students who are proficient enough to attend classes taught in Chinese, Filipino, Spanish, or Vietnamese as determined by the state administered proficiency examination or an interview with the site supervisors. All students must become completely fluent in their TL prior to completion of the program.)

2. Trainees are able to communicate effectively in English with LEP students and their parents.

Activities

1. Trainees attend bilingual cross-cultural core courses, which are taught completely in Chinese, Filipino, Spanish, or Vietnamese.

2. All communication between faculty and trainees in offices, during meetings, is in Chinese, Filipino, Spanish, or Vietnamese.

3. In their practical experiences, trainees work with LEP students and their parents.

Culture

1. The trainee is knowledgeable of general cultural characteristics of non-European American families including lifestyles, family structures, and community support systems.

2. The trainee understands the relevance of non-European American child rearing practice in the students' cognitive, emotional, and social development.

3. The trainee is aware of cultural conflicts resulting from ethic differences that may affect the students' self-image and thus influence their emotional and social development.

4. The trainee institutes a teaching process that takes into account the impact of cultural conflicts on the students' performance.

5. The trainee assesses and interprets observed classroom behavior in terms of different non-European American cultural norms.

6. The trainee demonstrates a knowledge of the ethnic, religious, and socioeconomic factors which are part of parents' dynamics, affect parental access to community resources, and influence the counseling process.

7. The trainee understands the acculturation process of culturally diverse individuals into the mainstream of American society.

8. The trainee implements techniques to facilitate the integration of LEP students into American schools.

9. The trainee is knowledgeable of different types of handicapping conditions and their interaction with sociocultural and linguistic variables.

Activities

1. Through reading, guest lectures, and class discussions in EDSE 179, EDSE 230, EDSE 216, EDSE 224, EDSE 228, EDSE 298C, the trainees

will acquire an awareness of different non-European American cultural characteristics.

2. Reading about cultural influences on cognitive styles are included in EDSE 224. Trainees evaluate exceptional students' cognitive styles in EDSE 215 and EDSE 298A. They utilize this information in teaching LEP students in EDSE 217 A and B.

3. Through a case study approach in EDSE 224, EDSE 228, and EDSE 298C, trainees become aware of the difficulties experienced by immigrants during the acculturation process.

4. Through reading, class discussions, and case studies in EDSE 228, trainees become aware of the relevancy of different non-European American cultures for the counseling process.

5. Through lecture and readings and case studies in EDSE 179, trainees will be able to observe and interpret the behavior of non-European American students in terms of cultural norms and select culturally appropriate classroom management techniques.

6. Through reading, guest lectures, and case studies in EDSE 230, EDSE 216, and EDSE 298B, trainees are able to select culturally appropriate instructional strategies for non-European American learning handicapped students.

Non-Discriminatory Assessment

1. Trainee demonstrates knowledge and understanding of the legal basis of bilingual bicultural education and special education in the United States. Trainee demonstrates critical understanding of relevant laws and regulations that impact the assessment and placement of LEP students.

2. The trainee is aware of the uses and limitations of current standard assessment techniques in regard to LEP students.

3. The trainee utilizes procedures and instruments in English, Chinese, Filipino, Spanish, and Vietnamese, and interprets the results using pluralistic multicultural norms when available. These instruments and procedures include commercially available tests, criterion reference tests, teacher prepared tests, diagnostic teaching, and standardized tests with multicultural and pluralistic norms as well as informal observations.

4. The trainee is aware of the influence of cognitive styles, cultural values, and language patterns of ethnic and minority groups on test performance.

5. The trainee formulates an accurate description of student ability based upon observation of academic performance in light of the students' cultural background.

Activities

1. Trainees become knowledgeable about the legal basis of bilingual bicultural education and special education through readings, lectures, and class discussions in EDU 224 and through application of rules and regulations to specific cases.

2. Trainees become aware of the relevant research concerning the use of specific assessment procedures with LEP students through readings, lectures, and class discussions in EDSE 107 and EDSE 298A. Trainees evaluates English, Chinese, Filipino, Spanish, and Vietnamese assessment procedures utilizing appropriate guidelines.

3. Trainees utilize informal and formal procedures in English, Chinese, Filipino, Spanish, and Vietnamese to assess LEP students in EDSE 298A, EDSE 215, EDSE 217, under supervision.

Language Assessment

1. The trainee understands the process of first and second language acquisition.

2. The trainee describes typical differences observed in the oral and written English language of speakers of Chinese, Filipino, Spanish, and Vietnamese in comparison to that of speakers of standard English.

3. The trainee distinguishes between the above differences in oral and written language and errors that may indicate deviant or deficient speech, and makes appropriate referrals.

4. The trainee selects nondiscriminatory assessment procedures in English and in Chinese, Filipino, Spanish, or Vietnamese to evaluate oral and written language development and proficiency.

5. The trainee uses the information gained to help to determine the LEP students' most appropriate and least restrictive educational setting.

6. The trainee is aware of how nonverbal behaviors of LEP students may lead to miscommunication between students and teachers.

Activities

1. Trainees study the process of first and second language acquisition in reading, lectures, and class discussion in EDSE 102.

2. In readings, lectures, and class discussions in EDSE 102 and EDSE 298D, trainees become knowledgeable about typical errors observed in the English and non-English language acquisition.

3. Trainees administer, score, and interpret English and Chinese, Filipino, Spanish, or Vietnamese language assessment instruments in EDSE 102 and EDSE 298D.

4. Trainees utilize these instruments in EDSE 217B to evaluate the development of student's oral and written language.

5. Trainees review research and critiques of English and Chinese, Filipino, Spanish, or Vietnamese language assessment procedures in EDSE 102 and EDSE 298D.

Instructional Strategies

1. The trainee utilizes bilingual/bicultural materials and strategies to improve the bilingual development of LEP students.

2. The trainee applies instructional strategies in light of cultural, socioeconomic, and language factors influencing learning.

3. The trainee plans, designs, and implements special education programs for LEP students in accordance with legislative requirements and guidelines.

4. The trainee utilizes ESL methods to foster the English language proficiency of LEP students.

Activities

1. Trainees study ESL methods in EDSE 290B.

2. Through lectures, readings, and class discussions in all courses in the bilingual cross-cultural core, trainees become aware of the non-English language materials that could be used with LEP students.

3. Trainees adapt English language materials for LEP students in EDSE 230, EDSE 216, EDSE 217 A and B, and EDSE 298B.

4. Trainees study culturally and linguistically appropriate instructional strategies in EDSE 216 and EDSE 230.

5. Trainees apply their knowledge of cultural and linguistic factors when selecting intervention and instructional strategies in their two practice experiences EDSE 217 A and B.

Counseling, Consultation, Advocacy, and Referral

1. Trainee provides nonbiased counseling to parents of LEP students.

A. The trainee adapts the counseling process to the ethnic, religious, and socioeconomic realities of the parents.

B. The trainee explains the implications of bilingual and special education legislation and regulations to the parents.

C. The trainee assesses those factors limiting the participation of non-European American parents in the educational decision-making process and develops strategies for overcoming them.

D. The trainee assists parents in understanding their children's learning problems, strengths, and weaknesses.

E. The trainee provides parents with information about available community resources and facilitates referrals.

F. The trainee assists the parents to collaborate at home with the instructional and management techniques utilized in the school.

2. The trainee consults with nonbilingual professionals who impact with students in order to interpret students' behavior, explain significance of test results, assist in the selection of appropriate nonbiased remedial and intervention procedures, advise about placement when necessary, and explain the implications of bilingual and special education legislation and regulations.

Activities

1. In readings, lectures, and class discussion in EDSE 228 and EDSE 298E, trainees become knowledgeable about the community resources available to LEP students, factors that impede the participation of parents in the educational decision-making process, and the specific ways in which different non-European American cultural factors affect the counseling process.

2. Trainees visit and volunteer in agencies that provide services to LEP students and their parents in EDSE 298E.

3. In EDSE 228 trainees select appropriate referrals for the LEP student and their parents presented in case studies.

4. Parents of LEP students discuss their experiences in EDSE 298E and EDSE 228.

5. Techniques for advocating rights of LEP students and their parents are presented in EDSE 228.

6. Trainees practice counseling, consulting, and advocacy techniques in role playing exercises in EDSE 228 and EDSE 298E.

Classroom Management

1. The trainee is aware of cultural influences on behavior.

2. The trainee appreciates the problems immigrant and refugee students experience while having to adjust to schools in which they are taught in an unfamiliar teaching style in a language they do not understand.

3. The trainee evaluates classroom behavior of LEP students in terms of cultural norms.

4. The trainee adapts techniques for helping students with emotional and behavioral problems to students' cultural characteristics.

Activities

1. In EDSE 179 trainees become knowledgeable about the effects of culture on behavior and the adjustment problems of immigrant and refugee students.

2. Trainees apply their knowledge of different non-European American cultural characteristics when evaluating the behavior of students presented in case studies and selecting appropriate intervention strategies and techniques in EDSE 179.

Professional Development

For those teachers who obtained degrees from institutions that did not focus on urban centers or those who completed their programs some time ago, staff development is critical. Marrapoli Guzman (1992), in her report for the fund for New York City public education, notes that ongoing professional development is critical to the success of a new program. They are:

1. decision-making

2. kick-off event

3. preservice professional development

4. one-to-one coaching and mentoring

These components have application to all professional development initiatives. Their applications to development and implementation of a program to meet the need of special educators who are charged with responsibility of the identification and instruction of special needs in students who represent a variety of linguistic and cultural backgrounds discussed below:

1. *Decision-Making.* This is the initial step in process. It is critical that all individuals involved in the identification and instruction of linguistically and culturally diverse students have a stake in the program. This should be a comprehensive needs' assessment to ascertain what the staff members want, and expanded discussions on how to meet these goals. This can be an open-ended or a specific check list. Staff members must learn that this is a team process, and they will be provided with support and resources in order to modify their current practices.

2. *Kick-off event.* This is designed to provide information and develop consensus among staff. Typically, an address from a keynote speaker that will provide staff with an enthusiastic and motivating presentation of major news. This can include nontraditional assessment, problems and issues regarding standardized tests, disproportionate numbers of African-American and Hispanic students in special education, appropriate instruction for linguistically and culturally diverse students, or other relevant types. It is hoped that this acts as a catalyst for change. It is important for staff members to recognize that this is the initial stage of the process. Too often the professional staff development is no more than a series of "one-shot" presentations. Regardless of the quality of the presentation and the prestige of the presenter, unless there is ongoing follow-up the presentation is useless and accomplishes little more that taking up valuable time that could be put to better uses.

3. *Preservice professional development.* Marrapoli Guzman (1992) defines this component as the training that is needed before the programs for children begins. For those involved in the identification, placement, and instructional process for special need students, this step will probably occur simultaneously with current programs. Essentially, the component deals with specific knowledge skills and attitudes teachers will need to implement the programs. I view this and the following component as similar in intent.

4. *Ongoing in-service professional development.* As noted above, this component and the previous component are aimed at providing the knowledge, skills, and attitudes necessary for a successful program. This may include full-day workshops, attendance at conferences, in-service courses that focus on specific types of careers (i.e., classroom management, reading instruction, assessment, etc.), as explained in the actual needs assessment of through ongoing communication with staff. For example, it may be apparent that staff members may need to gain information on social interaction, family structure, and the conception of disability for specific groups of students. Strategies suggested by Hill (1992) would be useful. They are listed below.

Social Interaction

1. Invite ethnic community leaders to participate in and observe special education meetings in order to help identify those processes that seem to be working—and why.

2. Poll parents as to which individuals or teams they find most comfortable to work with, and then observe the processes used by the groups.

3. Use those teams or individuals who are achieving better communication with parents to serve as district resources for staff development on communication issues.

4. Request permission from ethnic community groups to allow school personnel to participate in their meetings and other events so as to learn about specific cultural styles through participation.

Family Structures and Practices

1. Actively seek information from literature and from parents themselves about family structures and roles. Act on this knowledge by inviting and including the input of influential family members other than parents.

2. Actively seek information on culturally appropriate child rearing practices, especially on issues such as dependence/independence, regard/punishment, and group rights/individual rights.

3. Where child rearing practices differ significantly from mainstream practice or from school expectations, seek the advice of ethnic community leaders regarding the range of normative behavior. For example, if corporal punishment is used more frequently than is expected, try to develop a sense of what is considered abusive within the group's norms. Similarly, if dependence/independence of children appears to be an issue. Most often, professionals will have to strike a balance between the norms of the cultural group and the goals of students' special education program.

Finally, educators need to consider the recommendation of Ogbu (1992).

Prerequisites

- Recognize that there are different kinds of cultural/language differences and that the different types arise for different reasons or circumstances.

- Recognize that there are different types of minority groups and that the minority types are associated with the different types of cultural/language differences.

- Recognize that all minority children face problems of social adjustment and academic performance in school because of cultural/language differences. However, while problems faced by bearers of primary cultural differences are superficially similar to those of bearers of secondary cultural differences. The are fundamentally different. the reason lies in the difference in the relationship between the two types of cultural differences in white American mainstream culture.

Helping Children with Secondary Cultural/Language Differences. First, teachers and interventions must recognize that involuntary minority children come to school with cultural and language frames of reference that are not only different from but probably opposition to those of the mainstream and school. Second, teachers and interventionists should study the histories and cultural adaptations of involuntary minorities in order to understand the bases and nature of groups' cultural and language frames of reference as well as the childrens' sense of social identity. This knowledge will help them understand why these factors affect the process of minority schooling, particularly their school orientations and behaviors.

Third, special counseling and related programs should be used (a) to help involuntary minority students learn to separate attitudes and behaviors enhancing school success from those that lead to linear acculturation or acting "white," and (b) to help the students to avoid interpreting the former as a threat to their social identity and sense of security.

Fourth, programs are needed to increase students' adoption of the strategy of "accommodation without assimilation," "alternation model," or "playing the classroom game." The essence of this strategy is that students should recognize and accept the fact that they can participate in two cultural or language frames of reference for different purposes without losing their own cultural and language identity or undermining their loyalty to the minority community. They should learn to practice "when in Rome, do as the Romans do," without becoming Romans.

We have found from ethnographic studies (Ogbu and Hickerson, 1980) that whereas voluntary minority students try to learn to act according to school norms and expectations, involuntary minority students do not necessarily do so. Instead, they emphasize learning how to manipulate "the system," how to deal with or respond to white people and schools controlled by white people or their minority representatives. This problem should be addressed. A related approach that can be built into multicultural education programs is teaching the students their own responsibility for their academic performance and school adjustment.

Finally, society can help reorient minority youths toward more academic striving for school credentials for future employment by (a) creating more jobs in general, (b) eliminating the job ceiling against minorities, and (c) providing better employment opportunities for minorities.

The Role of the Involuntary Minority Community. The involuntary minority community can and should play an important part in changing the situation for three reasons. First, some of the needed changes can be most effectively brought about through community effort. Second, minority children do not succeed or fail only because of what schools do or do not do, but also because of what the community does. Third, our comparative research suggests that the social structure and relationship within the minority communities could be a significant influence of students' educational orientations and behaviors.

At this point in my research I suggest four ways in which the involuntary minority community can encourage academic striving and success among its children. One is to teach the children to have separate attitudes and behaviors that lead to academic success from attitudes and behaviors that lead to a loss of ethnic identity and culture and language. This can be achieved partly by successful members of the group retaining their social membership in the community and not dissociating themselves from the neighborhood, labeling the less successful individuals "underclass," and so on.

Second, the involuntary minority community should provide the children with concrete evidence that its members appreciate and value academic success as much as they appreciate and value achievements in sports, athletics, and entertainment.

Third, the involuntary minority community must teach the children to recognize and accept the responsibility on the children for their school behavior and academic performance (Gibson, 1988).

Finally, the involuntary minority middle class needs to reevaluate and change its role vis-à-vis the community. I have discovered in research two contrasting models of middle-class relationship with minority community, which I suspect have differential effects on minority school success. The first model is, apparently, characteristic of voluntary minorities. Here, successful, educated, and professional individuals, such as business people, doctors, engineers, lawyers, social workers, and university professors, appear to retain their minority neighborhoods. Such people regard their accomplishments as a positive contribution to their community—a community, not just individual, achievement. The community, in turn, interprets their accomplishments in a similar manner. The successful members participate in community events where they interact with the youth and less successful adults informally and outside the official roles as representatives of the welfare, police, school district, or white-controlled companies. In this community, the middle class provides concrete evidence to young people that school success pays and that school success and economic and professional success in the wider society are compatible with collective identity and bona fide membership in the minority community.

In contrast, involuntary minorities seem to have a model that probably does not have much positive influence on schooling. Members of involuntary minorities seem to view professional success as "a ticket" to leave their community both physically and socially, to get away from those who have not "made it." People seek education and professional success, as it were, in order to leave their minority community. White Americans and their media reinforce this by praising those who have made their way out of the ghetto, barrio, or reservation. The middle-class minorities do not generally interpret their achievements as evidence of the "development" or "progress" of its members. The middle class may later return to or visit the community with "programs," or as "advocates" for those left behind or as representatives of white institutions. They rarely participate in community events where they interact outside these roles with the youth and the less successful community members. Thus, the involuntary minority middle class does not provide adequate concrete evidence to the youth and the less successful that school success leads to social economic success in later adult life. The involuntary minority middle class must rethink its role vis-à-vis minority youth. What is needed is for the middle class to go beyond programs, advocacy, and institutional representation to reaffiliate with the community socially (pp. 12–13).

Summary

The need to train teachers in issues related to linguistic and cultural diversity is critical, especially given the disproportionate numbers of minority group students in special education and the changing demographics. These competencies should be infused throughout the curriculum, not merely added as in the form of a course or courses. Moreover, schools need to develop and implement systematic professional development programs in order to insure that all staff are prepared to meet this challenge.

7

Parents as Partners

Kroth (1985) has formulated a hypothesis regarding the interaction between home and school. He states that "cooperative home-school programs will accelerate pupils' academic behaviors and decrease undesirable social behaviors" (p. 41). It appears that this is a reasonable hypothesis for all educators, in particular those working with a culturally and linguistically diverse population. Also, as special educators, they are responsible for individual education program (IEP) meetings, in addition to traditional parent-teacher conferences. This section will discuss these and other issues that pertain to the development and implementation of an effective communication system between school and home.

General Guidelines

The field of special education is replete with technical jargon. Too often special education teachers employ these terms when discussing a student's difficulty during a meeting with parents. Rather than getting their point across to parents, this approach simply sets up a barrier to communication (McNamara, 1979). It is imperative that special education resource room teachers use jargon-free language when talking with parents. Jargon is simply ineffective because the listener may not understand what one is saying, and so the purpose of the meeting is lost. It is far better to attempt to describe terms in such a way that the parent will have examples of the specific behaviors and tasks in which their child is engaging. Parents must feel that the teacher has their best interest in mind. The manner in which one builds this type of trusting relationship will depend on one's particular style. However, there are a number of strategies to consider. Margolis and Brannigan (1986, pp. 72, 73) list eight of them:

1. *Accept parents as they are and do not try to induce fundamental changes.* Trying to change parents in some basic way communicates that something is wrong with them. For example, it would be a mistake to attempt to convince parents who are ardent supporters of the "back-to-basics movement" that a values clarification curriculum ismore important to children. In conflict situations especially, the less one's tries tochange broad-based philosophical beliefs of people, the greater one's ultimatechance of influencing them. At a later point in time, when trust is high, parents maydemonstrate their readiness to change by asking for assistance in learning newconcepts or skills.

2. *Listen carefully and empathetically for the cognitive and emotional content of the parents' message.* Teachers must give their complete, undivided, uninterrupted attention and must communicate that they understand. Statements should be short and to the point, using fresh words to summarize the parents' thoughts and feelings.

3. *Help parents feel comfortable and share information and resources with them, when legally permissible.* Small talk about mutual interests or experiences unrelated to the issues of contention and a symbolic "cup of coffee" frequently help parents feel more comfortable. Providing help and requesting legitimate assistance from parents establishes natural trust-building opportunities. Sharing information, resources, and ideas is a powerful process in building trust. On the other hand, evading requests for information or obscuring pertinent facts immediately creates the impression that one is hiding something important and heightens distrust and defensiveness.

4. *Prepare for meetings by studying pertinent materials beforehand so that a high level of knowledge will be apparent at the right moment.* Parents need to trust not only the teacher's objectives but also his or her knowledge and professional competency. It is critical that the teacher share relevant information at natural opportunities without lecturing, dominating, or conveying the slightest attitude of superiority. A few well-chosen comments or questions, devoid of technical information or relevant details, will create doubts about one's competency and interest.

5. *Focus on the parent's hopes, aspirations, concerns, and needs.* Parents' negative feelings toward school personnel usually arise from fear that their child's welfare is being jeopardized. Unilaterally setting agendas for parents, rather than focusing on their concerns, only intensifies distrust and resistance. It is natural to like someone who is interested in one's concerns. Attending to parents' concerns communicates caring.

6. *Keep one's word.* This is a simple rule, but is sadly often forgotten. If one promises a return telephone call at two o'clock, one should make it on time. Making the call promptly communicates respect and reliability.

7. *Allow parents' expertise to shine.* Parents are knowledgeable about many aspects of their child's development. Asking for their opinions, inviting them to comment on whether or not the student's behavior in school is representative of his or her behavior at home, and asking if one's viewpoints or suggestions appear to make sense to them (for example, "I was wondering if you have any thoughts about what I just said. If so, I'd appreciate your sharing them with me") facilitate trust and help and, establish the teacher as someone who values them. Providing knowledgeable answers in response to questions is desirable if it does not take the form of pontification, intimidation (for example, through the use of jargon, such as "perceptual problems," "haptic," "scaled scores," "stanines"), or unnecessary complexity. Asking parents to share their particular expertise communicates respect as long as they perceive the request to be both legitimate and timely.

8. *Be there when needed.* If parents have a legitimate need to see the teacher, the teacher should do everything reasonable to meet them as soon as possible, even if it creates a slight inconvenience.

Perl (1995) suggests developing relationship skills that can improve parent's conferences. He discusses six skills. They are: (1) genuine caring, (2) building rapport, (3) listening, (4) empathizing, (5) reflecting affect, and (6) clarifying statements. A checklist for self-monitoring is provided below (p. 31).

My Level of Competence (check one)

Skills	Adequate	Needs Improvement Goals
Caring		E.g., I will monitor my reactions, with parents from each meeting.
Building Rapport		E.g., I offer coffee or water to parents before each conference.
Listening		E.g., I will respons more often to concerns that express to me.
Empathizing		E.g., I will notice parents' nonverbal cues to help in perceiving their feelings.
Reflecting Affect		E.g., I will more often reflect feelings I perceive parents to be expressing.
Clarifying Statements		E.g., I will use clarifying statements when these can help parents improve their focus in conferences.

In addition to establishing a trusting relationship, the special educator will need to engage in specific tasks. They include attending the IEP conference, attending parent-teacher conferences, and developing ongoing communication. The remainder of this section will discuss each of these topics.

The IEP Conference

The purpose of this conference is to incorporate parental ideas into the student's educational program and to apprise parents of the teacher's focus for the year. The teacher would be wise to consult with, or have present, regular classroom teachers who are involved with the student. Much can be done prior to, during, and after the conference to make parents feel that they are productive members of the team (McNamara, 1986).

Before the Conference. Before developing or updating the IEP, the teacher should schedule a group parent meeting. The major purpose of such a meeting is to explain the purpose of the IEP and to inform parents of their legal rights. This meeting can also acquaint the parents with the format used by the school district. Letting parents know the rationale for the conference and the delivery of services provided for in the IEP will help establish open lines of communication. Often parents sign the IEP signifying their approval of the program, only to find that they are not receiving appropriate related services that are provided for under the law. Obviously, this situation does little to build up a trusting relationship between the home and the school. Being clear, precise, and up-front with the parents will pay high dividends in their ability to assist in carrying out the educational plan. Furthermore, it helps to allay any anxieties they may have regarding the parent-teacher conference.

If parents are gong to be able to offer meaningful input in the IEP, they must have time to formulate their ideas. Coming into a meeting and being asked for suggestions cannot be considered "meaningful input." Teachers should send a letter to parents (see form) at least two weeks prior to the conference requesting their ideas regarding the educational program of their child or adolescent. They should be provided with a stamped, addressed envelope. This lets them know that their input is important and valid, and will be considered by the teacher. If parents do not respond to the letter, a phone call can be made in an attempt to get this important information.

Parent Information Form

Student: _____

Teacher: _____

Date: _____

Parent Information Form *(continued)*

On *(fill in date)* we will meet to develop or update the individual educational plan for your child. Any ideas, thoughts, and concerns you have regarding the educational program for the year will be greatly appreciated. Feel free to use additional paper if necessary. Looking forward to seeing you.

Signed: _____

All of the above sets the stage for a productive meeting with parents.

During the Conference. Too often the school represents a threatening environment to parents of special children or adolescents. Teachers must do everything possible to make parents realize that they represent an integral component of their child's or adolescent's education. One suggestion is to have the meeting in a room other than the classroom. Classrooms are often filled with distracting stimuli, and rarely is there enough room for a table and three comfortable chairs. If the meeting must be in a classroom, the teacher should never sit behind the desk. This arrangement creates a physical, and perhaps psychological, barrier between the teacher and the parents. In addition, if any student's work is displayed, all of the student's work should be displayed. A circular table is preferred because no one is at the head and no one is therefore perceived as the most important or powerful. If at all possible, one should have refreshments available to add to the message that one is pleased to have the opportunity to plan this program with the parents.

After the Conference. Parents should be provided with an opportunity to evaluate the IEP conference. This practice has the advantage of providing the teacher with systematic feedback that he or she can use to improve performance and to better meet parental needs. The form developed by Hudson and Graham, 1978 (see below), is excellent for this purpose. As the authors note, the form can be adapted for individual school district needs. However, the philosophical intent of parent participation must be maintained.

Parent Form for Staffing Conference Feedback (from Hudson and Graham, 1978, pp. 309–18).

Student _____ Date _____

School _____ Grade _____

Parent(s) _____ Telephone _____

Home address _____

Parent Form for Staffing Conference Feedback *(continued)*

Staffing date _____ Time _____

Parents attending staffing conference _____

_____

_____

To the Parent: The purpose of this questionnaire is to obtain information that will assist the special service staff in improving communication between parents and professionals.

Recently you participated in a staffing conference concerning your child's needs. Based on your feelings about the conference, please respond to the following questions. For each question, check either "yes," "partially," or "no." If you wish to provide additional information, please print your statement. The last three questions are open-ended; therefore, you may respond to them with a written statement.

I. Administrative

A. Were you notified that your child has been referred for special education services prior to your invitation to attend the staffing conference?

( ) Yes   ( ) Partially   ( ) No

B. Was an effort made to have both parents participate in the staffing conference?

( ) Yes   ( ) Partially   ( ) No

C. Were you notified of the staffing conference early enough to ensure your participation?

( ) Yes   ( ) Partially   ( ) No

D. Was the staffing conference scheduled at a mutually agreed upon time and place?

( ) Yes   ( ) Partially   ( ) No

E. Were you told who would be attending the staffing conference?

( ) Yes   ( ) Partially   ( ) No

F. Were you informed of the purpose of the staffing conference?

( ) Yes   ( ) Partially   ( ) No

Parent Form for Staffing Conference Feedback *(continued)*

G. Were you told that you could invite outside professionals retained by you?

( ) Yes ( ) Partially ( ) No

H. Were you informed of due process procedures and your rights to appeal decisions?

( ) Yes ( ) Partially ( ) No

I. Were you provided a copy of the IEP?

( ) Yes ( ) Partially ( ) No

II. Professional

A. Were team members knowledgeable of your child's emotional and social behavior?

( ) Yes ( ) Partially ( ) No

B. Were team members knowledgeable of your child's academic status?

( ) Yes ( ) Partially ( ) No

C. Was a variety of service options discussed relative to your child's needs?

( ) Yes ( ) Partially ( ) No

D. Was the assessment information collected from a variety of sources;

( ) Yes ( ) Partially ( ) No

E. Was the assessment evaluation conducted by multidisiciplinary team?

( ) Yes ( ) Partially ( ) No

F. Do you feel that the test instruments used were culturally or racially discriminatory?

( ) Yes ( ) Partially ( ) No

G. Did the team justify any removal of your child from the regular classroom?

( ) Yes ( ) Partially ( ) No

III. Parental

A. Did you feel comfortable attending the staffing conference?

( ) Yes ( ) Partially ( ) No

Parent Form for Staffing Conference Feedback *(continued)*

B. Were you asked about your opinions?

( ) Yes   ( ) Partially   ( ) No

C. Did you feel free to contribute suggestions regarding your child's needs?

( ) Yes   ( ) Partially   ( ) No

D. Did the professional staff appear interested in what you had to say?

( ) Yes   ( ) Partially   ( ) No

E. Do you feel that the professional staff felt your participation was important?

( ) Yes   ( ) Partially   ( ) No

F. Were you provided ample time to express information that you felt to be relevant?

( ) Yes   ( ) Partially   ( ) No

G. Did you understand the IEP developed for your child?

( ) Yes   ( ) Partially   ( ) No

H. Did you feel that your child should have participated in the staffing conference?

( ) Yes   ( ) Partially   ( ) No

IV. General

A. Do you feel that the recommendations made were in the best interest of your child?

( ) Yes   ( ) Partially   ( ) No

B. Are you satisfied with the decision made at the staffing conference?

( ) Yes   ( ) Partially   ( ) No

C. Do you feel that support services other than those recommended are needed for your child's progress?

( ) Yes   ( ) Partially   ( ) No

D. Did you feel free to ask questions regarding the contributions, evaluation, and suggestions of the

1. classroom teacher?   ( ) Yes   ( ) Partially   ( ) No

2. Learning specialist or special teacher?   ( ) Yes   ( ) Partially   ( ) No

Parent Form for Staffing Conference Feedback (*continued*)

   3. special education
      representative or
      administration?   ( ) Yes   ( ) Partially   ( ) No

   4. assessment team member?   ( ) Yes   ( ) Partially   ( ) No

   5. school psychologist?   ( ) Yes   ( ) Partially   ( ) No

   6. _____?   ( ) Yes   ( ) Partially   ( ) No

E. At the conclusion of the staffing conference, how did you perceive
   your child's problems in view of your previous understanding?

   _____

   _____

   _____

   _____

F. Remarks

   _____

   _____

   _____

   If the IEP conference is to succeed, the special education teachers must
be able to communicate in clear, precise language.

   Teachers must transmit information to parents about the observable
academic and social behaviors emitted by their children or adolescents. For
example, rather than telling a parent that his or her child has an auditory
comprehension deficit, the teacher should note that the child has difficulty
understanding information when it is spoken. This kind of language provides
a much more accurate description of students' strengths and weaknesses. As
teachers, we tend to think that because we know the meaning of a term, that
the parent will also know it. However, teachers cannot assume that parents
will understand their terminology. After all, why should they?

   Teachers should also encourage parents to read all educational reports
in great detail. Every familiar word should be circled and discussed with the
teacher. Parents should tape-record or take written notes. This practice not
only provides them with a valuable record-keeping procedure that they can

refer to at a later date, but also provides them with a glossary of unfamiliar terms. Finally, the most important suggestions is that teachers encourage parents to assert themselves. Parents should never feel embarrassed to ask the teacher what is meant by a technical term—it is their right to know (McNamara, 1979).

Ongoing Activities

In addition to the activities noted above, teachers should develop ongoing activities that will enable them and the parents to keep in touch. They may include the following:

Periodic phone calls (focus on the positive)

Periodic notes to parents (again, try to be positive)

Monthly meetings

Home-school reinforcement systems (see Kroth, 1985, for specific details)

Breakfast meetings prior to school for working parents who may be overscheduled during the evening.

Parent-Teacher Conferences

The IEP conference should be viewed as the beginning of the communication process, not the end. The goal should be to increase parental involvement prior to the IEP conference, to communicate effectively during the conference, and to provide parents with opportunities to meet and talk throughout the school year. One way to provide these opportunities is to attend the traditional parent-teacher conferences. Much of what was stated above is applicable here. A few other tips are offered by the editors of *Academic Therapy* (1987, pp. 411–12):

- Mail a written note (it's better not to trust Johnny to deliver it) or call the parents to establish a firm conference date. When so many mothers are working outside the home, setting a time during the school day may be difficult. If so, check with your principal or district to determine policies on after school or evening conferences.

- Request a confirmation of the time, place, and date if you have used a written, mailed communication. (Nothing beats a mailed note over and beyond a telephone call.)

- Read the student's cumulative folder thoroughly. Be familiar with the vast array of tests that have been administered to the child. Double check. Are there any gaps that require updated testing in specific areas, e.g., math, oral reading, etcetera? If so, determine who will do the testing and when. You will need that information prior to your appointment with the parents.

- In addition to test results, set aside a folder showing school assignments from September through the conference date. Point out the ways in which these illustrate the student's strengths and weaknesses.

- Be positive. Start the conference with a description of an area in which the child has excelled. Then move into ongoing needs.

- A desk can become a barrier. Try to sit in a cluster for example, around a utility table, so that test results and work samples can be comfortably shared. Keep your language simple and nontechnical. It is an act of kindness to say to parents, "Please interrupt me at any time if I should use a term or make a statement that you do not understand."

- The conference should be a two-way dialogue. Engage the parents as much as possible. Get their observations on how Johnny and Susan react to school, learning, homework, friends. Listen! Be sure to let them know how much you value their opinions. Parents have much to offer and sometimes need to be reassured of the contribution they make to the youngster's well-being.

- When possible, have the child participate in the school conference.

- A conference should not last longer than one hour. Allow time to summarize and make recommendations for the coming year as well as suggestions for summer activities.

- If the physical set up makes it possible, a cup of coffee sets a warm, friendly tone. Kroth (1985, p. 73) cites a conference check list developed by the Parent Center in Albuquerque, New Mexico, that can be another useful way to prepare for the conference.

Preconference

_____ 1. Notify
- purpose, place, time, length of time allotted

_____ 2. Prepare
- review child's folder
- gather examples of work
- prepare materials

_____ 3. Plan agenda

_____ 4. Arrange environment
- comfortable seating
- eliminate distractions

Conference

_____ 1. Welcome
  • establish rapport

_____ 2. State
  • purpose
  • time limitations
  • note-taking
  • options for follow-up

_____ 3. Encourage
  • information sharing
  • comments
  • questions

Postconference

_____ 1. Review conference with child, if appropriate

_____ 2. Share information with other school personnel, if needed

_____ 3. Mark calendar for planned follow-up

Additional Concerns

The above may be successful with many parents of culturally and linguistically diverse students. However, the educators used to be cognizant of other issues that may arise. Klyanpur and Rao (1991) note that it is a particular challenge to strike a balance between services provided and the perceived needs of the family. They suggest that educators recognize the difference in family values among the students they serve. Parents need to be empowered by professionals who care and build supportive relationships, who respect families and who accept differences and build trust. The provision of specific services is insufficient in establishing relationships between home and school. Sileo, Sileo, and Prates (1996) outline general approaches for facilitating parent and family involvement for diverse learners.

    Parent education programs that improve parents' formal education (e.g., English as a second language, basic reading, mathematics, reasoning skills)

• increase parents' self-esteem and self-confidence;

• facilitate positive interactions with school professionals;

- broaden employment opportunities; and
- facilitate parent feelings of "being at home" in educational settings.

Parent education programs that are designed to increase parents' influence on their children's education

- ensure that schools are responsive to school and community values;
- give parents the opportunity to participate in the school's decision-making process;
- require that educators

    a) observe and participate in community activities,

    b) listen to parents' wants, hopes, and concerns to develop mutual understanding, and

    c) encourage parents to define desired change and to develop and action plan.

Awareness training programs that provide opportunities for role play and simulation

- increase parent confidence levels for interacting with school personnel
- facilitate parents' understanding of shared responsibility for children's education (e.g., training in individualized education program [IEP] process and for advocacy roles);
- teach new behaviors and skills needed to interact as educational team members (e.g., problem solving, critical thinking, and communication skills, such as active listening, self-disclosure);
- increase family interactions and participation in children's education (e.g., IEP participation, behavior management strategies, volunteering at school, assisting with homework;) and
- empower parents and extend leadership abilities in the educational community (e.g., school-community-based management, curriculum development committee, assisting with homework).

Training and employment of parents as paraeducators in bilingual and bicultural programs to

- include language and customs as a part of the curriculum;
- learn instructional strategies that can be used to benefit their own children at home; and
- increase the likelihood that parents will choose to further their education.

They also suggest that education examine the values of efficiency, independence, and equity in order to develop culturally sensitive strategies. They provide the chart below:

Western Culture/Values	Family Culture/Values	Strategies
Efficiency		
Value/use of time wisely; quality of task may be secondary	Efficient use of time not as important; OK to be late	Avoid scheduling parent-conferences too closely together
Direct approach; get right to the subject; solve problem	Indirect approach; discuss related issues; "talk story"	Avoid "quick fix"; respect of interaction
Tend to rush, fast paced	More slowly paced, need time to think	Slow pace of meetings with parents; allow "thinking time"
Independence		
Prefer to make own decisions	Interdependence, decisions are made as a family; natural family suports supports in place	Encourage extended family involvement; work with extended family members
Individual right to privacy of feelings	Strong family ties; open sharing of personal feelings; actions of individual reflect on entire family	Respect sense of family; identify cultural attitudes or religious beliefs toward disabilities
Parental responsibility for raising child	Extended family, shared responsibility of child-bearing	Identify authority figures. Respect deference to authority. Allow parents time to take decision to to others
Equity		
Parents are equal partners in team	Perceive professional as "above" family	Professionals need to be aware of an "read" parent perceptions; recognize parents as experts
Prefer active parent involvement (e.g., input at meetings, work with child at home)	Accept teachers' opinion. Teachers are experts	Decrease control of interaction; involve parents in planning, implementing, and monitoring programs

Western Culture/Values	Family Culture/Values	Strategies
Information sharing	Passive reception of information	Elicit wants, hopes, and concerns of parents; information sharing versus information giving and questions asking; use parent suggestions when possible; provide timely feedback
Democratic family decision-making	Matriarchal or patriarchal family structures	Respect lines of authority

Harry (1992) summarizes the most common features of participation of minority parents in special education program. They are:

1. Lower levels of involvement than white counterparts

2. Less awareness of special education procedures, rights, and available services

3. An expressed sense of isolation and helplessness

4. Low self-confidence in interaction with professionals

5. Stressful life circumstances that overwhelm parents

6. Need for logistical supports such as transportation, child care, and respite

7. Culturally based assumptions of noninterference on the part of parents in school matters

8. Professionals' implicit or explicit discouragement of parents' participation in the special education process (p. 100)

She suggests that educators must reach out to parents in order to minimize cultural dissonance and provide them with advocacy training if the gap between culturally different parents and school personnel be reduced. Harry's (1992) specific recommendations include:

• Restructuring parent-professional discourse

• Changing professional attitudes

It is critical to recognize that communication is not compliance. Parents must be partners in the decision-making process. Recent research (Harry,

Allen, and McLaughlin, 1995) cites deterrents to such a partnership. They include: (1) late notices and inflexible schedules; (2) limited time for conferences; (3) emphasis on documents, not participation; (4) the use of jargon; and (5) the structure of power. The authors note that if this is to succeed, professionals need "to relinquish stereotypical notions about families whose structure does not resemble the mainstream ideals" (p. 375). Finally, Dennis and Giangreco (1996) provide useful suggestions for dealing with families in a more culturally sensitive way.

Seek help from "cultural interpreters" before the interview

- Have someone from the community determine whether the interview protocol "fits" in the community.

- Become aware of the social interaction norms of the community, so that initial impressions will be appropriate.

- Have a community liaison worker who knows the specific cultural patterns of families within that neighborhood make initial contacts and present realistic choices to parents.

Carefully ascertain literacy and language status of family members

- Adjust the interview style for nonreaders and speakers of other languages.

- Consider that family members may not be literate in their native language or English.

- Advise families who speak another language in the home that they are entitled to the service of an interpreter, rather than just asking if they wish one, since they may decline, thinking that it is too much to ask.

- Be knowledgeable of skills needed by educators to work successfully with interpreters.

- Do not use siblings or other students as interpreters.

- Familiarize the interpreter ahead of time with any documents that must be presented at the conference.

- Team members should address both the parents and the interpreter as they speak, rather than facing only the interpreter.

Involve family members in planning interviews

- Let families know that their input is important by including them in scheduling a date, time, and location of the interview, and determining who should attend.

- Consider meeting with parents at their places of employment during lunch or right after work, at a community center, at another agency location, or in the family home at flexible times so that the parent feels comfortable.

- Be aware that some families may be very uncomfortable with school personnel visiting their homes for various reasons (e.g., their undocumented status, embarrassment about the condition of their home, previous bad experiences with school personnel).

- Consider whether parents might feel intimidated by too many professionals, and adjust the number as appropriate.

- Allow for inclusion of "significant others" (e.g., extended family).

- Be sensitive to problems that may arise when both parents cannot be present.

- Consider meeting with several families at one time. Family members may feel more comfortable sharing information within a close network of family members and neighbors.

- Plan to involve a team member who knows the family or can establish rapport. If the interviewer is from the same culture, he or she can better individualize the information in terms of use of narrative language and vocabulary.

Preview the interview with family members

- Let family members know that they will be respected and that if something annoys them, they can say so.

- Be sensitive to what parents would like you to do. Would they be more comfortable with a social visit, or would they like you to be more businesslike?

- Put yourself in the learner role. Acknowledge your own ignorance, and ask for ideas or questions the family may have to improve the interview.

- Follow the parents' lead right from the start, and allow them to establish the parameters of the interview.

Be flexible and responsive to the family's interaction style

- Access the situation; expect that every situation is going to be different.

- Allow the family to tell stories about the child. Parents need time to think when answering the broad, sweeping questions. Their answers may not be specific or clear. Telling stories is one way they can clarify their thoughts on their priorities for their child. Stories can establish a common understanding of the background, family history, and relationships in order to build trust.

Adapt the time frame to meet the needs of the family

- Be prepared to spend time with the family before and after the family interview.

- Be sensitive to the need for some families to confer with other family members and think through important educational decisions over time.

- Be aware that in some families it is important to "break bread" with one another and first "connect." It may take months before a family is comfortable with school personnel and willing to divulge the level of information that is requested by the system.

Carefully examine the nature of the questions you ask

- Confidentiality needs to be highlighted and emphasized as much as possible. Discretion is critical; loss of confidentiality can lead to a failure to work with the team, and ultimately to the child's losing out.

- There are things you don't ask. A family member may be offended if someone were to ask questions without his or her understanding why they wanted to know. It might be a very spiritual or personal subject, and may be perceived as having nothing to do with how their child is going to do in school.

- Issues of shame and guilt could arise if the parents feel blamed or if the child's problems are possibly related to parental substance abuse or other behaviors.

- Because some parents who may receive public assistance feel that their lives are constantly being invaded, informing them of the fact that they do not have to answer questions that are too sensitive is critical.

- Ask family members for feedback regarding questions that are not appropriate for future use with other families.

- Continually focus the conversation on what will benefit the child, because across the culture groups, what is most imporant is the welfare of their children.

Teachers' Perceptions of Rating an Early Literacy Portfolio*

Jacqueline Jones
Edward Chittenden

The Early Literacy Portfolio's Scale.   After the Early Literacy Portfolio had been developed and implemented, a six-point developmental scale was created by South Brunswick teachers in consultation with Educational Testing Service researchers. The scale was constructed around six stages that characterize the early development of children's abilities to read and write. Several instruments influenced the scale's design. These include Holdaway's (1979) analysis of early reading stages, Clay's (1985) work on reading assessment, and a "reading code" that was developed in 1985 by teachers at Central Park East Elementary School in New York City to summarize children's progress. In addition, the Reading Scale of the Primary Language Record (Barrs, Ellis, Hester and Thomas, 1989) was particularly important because it constituted one of the few examples of an assessment that combined observational records and a rating scale. These and other sources were reviewed and modified to fit within the South Brunswick curriculum model. [See supplement for the South Brunswick Early Literacy Portfolio's Scale.]

Each stage of the scale is couched in terms of what children *can* do, as reflected in the records and work samples in the portfolios. The scale spans

*Additional copies of this report can be ordered from:
Center for Performance Assessment, Educational Testing Service, Mail Stop 11-P, Rosedale Road, Princeton, NJ 08541-0001 • (609) 734-5521

the period from entry into kindergarten through completion of the second grade. During that period, most children are expected to progress from he emergent stages of levels 1 and 2, through the two beginning stages of 3 and 4, to the independent stages of levels 5 and 6. Children's strategies and abilities to make sense of print were the scale's focus. The scale is not intended to rate broader dimensions of literacy, such as the child's interests in reading or general language proficiency. As stated in Draft 5 of the Early Literacy Portfolio's scale, *The scale does not attempt to rate children's interests or attitudes regarding reading, nor does it attempt to summarize what literature may mean to the child. Such aspects of children's literacy development are summarized in other forms.* Ratings of children's reading and writing achievement are made by teachers at the middle and at the end of the school year, and are based solely on the Early Literacy Portfolio documents.

The district realized that successful implementation of the Early Literacy Portfolio would require more than a mandate that a series of work samples be collected by teachers and rated twice a year. If the Early Literacy Portfolio and its scale were to function as a credible assessment process, methods of "checking up" on the process needed to be designed. The question of comparable use of the portfolio assessment is addressed in two ways: a common set of procedural guidelines and portfolio scale meetings.

Procedural Guidelines. A common set of procedural guidelines has been developed for each component of the assessment system. These guidelines, which are fairly specific in describing how and when the performance documents are to be collected, allow teachers flexibility in determining how best to manage the data collection within the context of their particular classroom routines. Staff are trained in the meaning and use of these guidelines. The continuing challenge is to design procedures that promote comparability across classrooms without becoming too prescriptive or burdensome. As a rule of thumb, Teacher A should be able to read and interpret the documents in Teacher B's folders so that they can be used reliably for ratings.

Portfolio Scale Meetings. Each year the district conducts meetings at which teachers across the district read, discuss, and rate their colleague's Early Literacy Portfolios. Working in pairs, teachers are presented with the portfolio of a child they do not know, and rated the contents of the portfolio.

The Teachers. Sixty-three of the sixty-four primary-level teachers in South Brunswick's seven schools were interviewed for this study. The variation among teachers in years of classroom experience was considerable. At the time of the interview, 17 percent were new to teaching and were in the midst of their first or second year of instructional practice. Teachers with three to nine years experience constituted 40 percent of the sample, and those with ten or more years of experience made up 43 percent of the group.

Experience with the Portfolio Assessment Process. For twenty-nine percent of the teachers interviewed, this was their first year of using the portfolio. This group included eleven new teachers and seven experienced teachers, all of whom were new to the portfolio process either because they had been recently assigned to a primary grade or because they were recently hired by the district. Sixteen percent of the teachers were in their second year of portfolio use. The remaining fifty-five percent of the teachers had three or more years of experience with the portfolio. Many in this last group had served on the committee responsible for the early versions of the portfolio assessment and for its major revisions.

At the time of the interviews, approximately one-third of the teachers in the sample were teaching a "combined" class, such as kindergarten/first grade or first/second grades. The remaining two-thirds taught "straight" kindergarten, first, or second grades. Although the portfolio was designed for the K–2 grades, a prekindergarten teacher was included in the interviews because she had adapted components to that grade level.

Data Collection. All teachers were individually interviewed concerning their use, interpretation, and evaluation of the Early Literacy Portfolio and its scale. The interviews, conducted by three staff members from Educational Testing Service, generally ranged from thirty to forty-five minutes in duration and took place within the school buildings, during school hours. Teachers were informed that their responses would remain confidential and that the interview was intended to elicit their evaluation of the Early Literacy assessment project as well as to conduct research on portfolio assessment. Each teacher was asked to bring one or two "typical" portfolios to the interview. Teacher participation was voluntary, and substitute teachers were hired to cover the classrooms of some participants.

The Interview. The interview was divided into three sections. In the first, and longest portion, teachers were asked to conduct a "walk through" of the portfolio's components, and they were probed for what the various documents told them about the child. The second section consisted of questions concerning the management of the portfolio, asking teachers how they went about collecting and organizing the documents.

The third section of the interview, which is the focus of the present paper, directed teachers' attention to the developmental scale and to the rating process. These questions were generally introduced by *I'd like you to think next about the scale and the process of rating the portfolios.* The teachers were then asked:

- *What do you think of the rating process? Of rating all the children in your class? Probes: Is this useful? Not Useful?*

- *How did you learn to use the scale?*

- *Was there any benefit to the district meetings where teachers exchange and rate each other's portfolios? If so, what is the benefit?*

Given the open-ended nature of the questions, teachers could talk mainly about what was especially salient or important to them about the scale and the district's meetings. In some cases they related their comments about the scale to the documents in the portfolios they had brought to the meeting, illustrating why a particular portfolio might be rated for "3," for example. Interviewers took detailed notes during the course of the interview; immediately following each session, time was set aside for the interviewer to complete the notes as necessary. As much as possible, the notes attempted to capture the teacher's language.

Data Analysis. As the first step in data analysis, categories were developed that reflected the specific content of the teachers' remarks. These categories were intended to be descriptive, for the purpose of grouping together statements that focused on similar features or qualities of the scale. Following initial development of categories, responses were sorted independently by the authors to check on clarity and agreement.

The second step in data analysis involved grouping the descriptive categories into larger categories reflecting different types of uses of the scale, or different types of benefits. The purpose was to move from the discrete descriptive categories to somewhat more inclusive categories, which necessarily called for greater interpretation. This analysis was not confined to responses to a single question, but could take into account other comments made by the teachers in other sections of the interview, if they shed light on what was meant. As in the first step, subsequent to initial development of categories, the responses were analyzed independently by the authors. Discrepancies were then discussed and resolved through reanalysis, sometimes with the assistance of a third researcher who had been one of the interviewers. Finally, agreement was reached on the coding of all responses.

Results are presented in two parts. The first part describes the teachers' evaluations of the rating process and the scale. The benefits and limitations noted by the teachers reveal their views of the nature of the relationship between scores from the scale and the documents in the portfolio. The second part of the results describes teachers' comments on how they learned to use the scale and their evaluations of the district meetings.

Teachers' Evaluations of the Rating Process. The great majority of responding teachers indicated that the rating process and scale were useful. However, this general agreement concerning the scale's usefulness did not preclude some variation among the teachers in the types of reasons they offered for finding the scale helpful. As reported below, some interviewees saw the scale as an essential piece of the portfolio project; others viewed it simply as a beneficial, if somewhat nonessential, adjunct. A few teachers found little value in the scale or rating process, describing the measure as "not useful." However, even these teachers did not indicate that the scale was in any way incompatible with their own student evaluations or use of the portfolio documents.

Benefits of the Scale. Since the interview questions about the scale were open-ended, teachers' responses covered a broad range of impressions. Figure 1 depicts the teachers' perspectives of the principal functions of the scale; the teachers' comments have been categorized accordingly. Some teachers described more than one function or quality of the scale. Therefore, the total percentage of responses amounts to over 100 percent.

The most frequently mentioned benefit was the scale's value in helping teachers discern patterns in children's learning—*Highlights Patterns of Development.* Teachers described this benefit as assisting them in assessing the progress of an individual child. They noted that reviewing a child's portfolio and using the scale as a reference helped them see progress in the child's work over the course of the year or, in some cases, from grade to grade. Teachers reported that the scale, *Let me focus on progress,* and *I find it interesting that the children have really grown.* Several also stated that the scale was particularly useful for identifying children whose lack of progress indicated the need for extra attention: *The scale serves as a red flag for at risk children.* Along with seeing patterns in individual development, some teachers referred to the scale's value in providing an overview of their class: *I like the scale because when I look at my class I can see the children's levels . . . [the scale] tells me the range.*

The second most frequently mentioned function placed emphasis on the process of review that was an integral aspect of using the scale. In the category *Confirms of Enhances the Process of Review,* the teachers' comments stressed the value of systematically reviewing all of a child's work samples, a process prompted by the requirement that ratings should be based on evidence within the portfolios. In that respect, the scale served as a prompt: *It's useful . . . makes me think about what this child did in all areas. A good review process.* Another stated *It makes me look at everything in the folder. Puts meaning to the folder when I scale it.* Teachers also expressed the belief that the review

Figure 1: Teachers' Evaluation of the Rating Process
(based on 60 teachers)

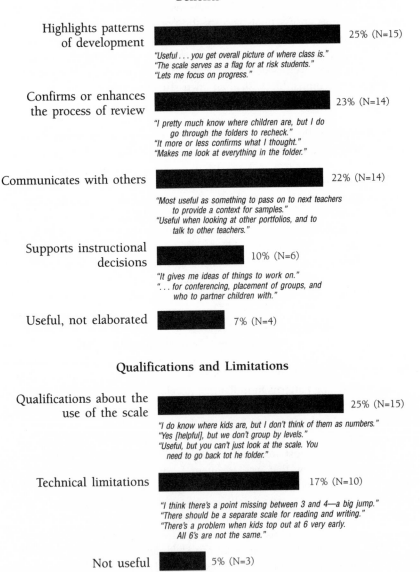

Benefits

Highlights patterns
of development
    25% (N=15)

"Useful . . . you get overall picture of where class is."
"The scale serves as a flag for at risk students."
"Lets me focus on progress."

Confirms or enhances
the process of review
    23% (N=14)

"I pretty much know where children are, but I do
go through the folders to recheck."
"It more or less confirms what I thought."
"Makes me look at everything in the folder."

Communicates with others
    22% (N=14)

"Most useful as something to pass on to next teachers
to provide a context for samples."
"Useful when looking at other portfolios, and to
talk to other teachers."

Supports instructional
decisions
    10% (N=6)

"It gives me ideas of things to work on."
". . . for conferencing, placement of groups, and
who to partner children with."

Useful, not elaborated
    7% (N=4)

Qualifications and Limitations

Qualifications about the
use of the scale
    25% (N=15)

"I do know where kids are, but I don't think of them as numbers."
"Yes [helpful], but we don't group by levels."
"Useful, but you can't just look at the scale. You
need to go back tot he folder."

Technical limitations
    17% (N=10)

"I think there's a point missing between 3 and 4—a big jump."
"There should be a separate scale for reading and writing."
"There's a problem when kids top out at 6 very early.
All 6's are not the same."

Not useful
    5% (N=3)

0   5   10   15   20   25
Percentage of Teachers

196

process gave them reassurance and confirmation that their everyday appraisals of children's reading were on track: *It more or less confirms what I thought . . . very few surprises.* Or sometimes they noted that it was an occasion for checking and perhaps modifying their own interpretations: *Some kids are very easy to place and I don't need to look closely at the portfolio. For other children, I have to really analyze the portfolio.*

The third most frequently mentioned benefit noted by the interviewees, *Communicates with Others*, concerned the scale's value for communicating with other teachers and, occasionally, with administrators or parents. The focus of comments in this category was on the score itself, rather than on the rating process that produced the score. Several teachers mentioned the value of the score as part of the portfolio package that they sent on the child's next teacher: *Most useful as something to pass on to the next teacher to provide a context for the work samples.* For some this seemed to be a primary purpose: *The scale is more for the next teacher.* Other teachers commented on the usefulness of receiving scores from the previous teacher, suggesting that it served as a point of entry for looking at portfolio information: *[The scores] at least give you a point at which to start.* Or, from a first grade teacher, *I look at where they were at the end of kindergarten.* A few teachers also noted that the scores, along with portfolio information, played a useful part in conferences with colleagues concerning decisions about a particular child or in meetings with parents.

A fourth, less frequently noted benefit was *Supports Instructional Decisions.* Teachers noted that, with respect to individual children, the scale alerted them to *things I need to work on.* However, it was unclear from their comments whether they were referring to the scale's numerical value or to the behavioral descriptors that delineated each scale point. Some teachers also suggested that the scale played some role in their decision about forming instructional groups.

Qualifications and Limitations of the Scale. While the great majority of the teachers felt that the scale served some useful functions for assessment, many of these same teachers also commented upon the limitations of the rating process and scale. As indicated in Figure 1, there were two types of limitations: one concerned the meager information value of the developmental scale score when compared to evidence within the actual portfolio's documents; the second limitation concerned technical problems in the scale's design.

As illustrated in Figure 1, one-fourth of the responding teachers suggested that although the scale had beneficial uses, it was only an indicator. The interviewees emphasized that "real data" resided in the samples of student work that make up the contents of the portfolio. Several reiterated the view that the documents in the portfolio, rather than the scale's score itself, constituted the critical source of information about a child: *The ratings are not as important as the samples,* or *I use the actual things in the folder.* Others were explicit in maintaining a distance between the ratings as an estimate of student progress and their own sense of the children's growth; one does not replace the other. One teacher said she considered the scores when planning or evaluating instructional groups, but she then emphasized, *I don't have these numbers in my head.* Another stated: *I do know where my kids are, but I don't think of them as numbers.*

The other sorts of limitations mentioned by teachers were more technical in nature. Some second-grade teachers observed that the scale "tops out" at their level and is, thus, not useful for monitoring the progress of children who have md into the "Independent" stages of reading, which mark the upper point of the scale. Furthermore, at the lower range, some kindergarten teachers expressed misgivings about the scale's restricted focus on children's responses to print, feeling that it missed much that was important about children's early language development. Finally, there were recommendations directed toward clarifying the language of the scale and to the issue of whether early writing should be rated separately from reading.

Methods by which Teachers Acquired Knowledge of the Scale. The preceding analysis was based on teachers' responses to interview questions concerning the usefulness of the rating process and the portfolio's scale. Teachers were also asked: (1) to describe how they had learned to use the scale and (2) to evaluate the district's annual portfolio scale meeting at which teachers exchanged and rated samples of each others' portfolios. Responses to these two questions were examined for additional evidence bearing upon the teachers' interpretations of the scale and their perception of its role in portfolio assessment. Results are reported below.

Learning to Use the Scale. Responding teachers indicated that they had learned to use the scale through both formal training and informal, on-the-job experience. As reflected in Figure 2, fifty percent of the teachers indicated that *District Workshops and Meetings* had provided important knowledge on the use of the rating scale. One teacher responded, *South Brunswick gives workshops all the time. They* [the district] *did a good thing.* The district workshops had been settings in which teachers were introduced to the portfolio's documents and scale, and learned about its implementation and applications. In some cases, these were summer language arts workshops that included general training on the use of the early literacy portfolio. Other meetings that teachers mentioned were grade-level staff meetings in which "same-grade" teachers from the different schools came together to review the district's assessment and instructional practices. For the most part, the teachers felt that such training opportunities were worthwhile and indeed were an essential part of district's support for portfolio assessment. Many felt that more training should be available, especially for newer staff.

Forty-four percent of the responding teachers indicated that their working knowledge of the scale had been acquired primarily through a second category, *On-the-job experience and working with others.* Some talked about their struggles to master the ratings on their own, *I read it and practiced; tore my hair out and changed numbers several times. I learned just by using it. I find it cumbersome, although I'm getting better at it.* Many of these respondents also emphasized the critically important role of their colleagues, in their building, as a source of help or feedback for interpreting and determining the ratings. They reported that meeting with other teachers in their schools and discussing the portfolio contents was the primary method of learning to use the scale. Another teacher stated, *I had one of the other teachers explaining it to me. I did it, and we went over it. I listened to the kindergarten the first grade teachers doing theirs. I gave them some of my children and asked them if I rated correctly.*

Six teachers who had worked on the portfolio development team stated that the basis of their knowledge about the scale came from *Participating in the portfolio development committee.* Only four teachers reported that they initially learned to use the rating scale through *Participating in portfolio scale meetings.* It should be noted that some teachers also reported using a combination of methods to learn how to use the scale. In sum, the teachers had learned to use the scale by attending workshops, by working with colleagues, and through trial and error. As one pointed out, *I went to the workshops, but the fine tuning and practice came with my peers* [in the school building].

Evaluating of the Portfolio Scale Meetings. As part of the interview, teachers were also asked to evaluate the district's annual portfolio scale meeting. Typically, these meetings brought together a sample of kindergarten through second grade teachers from different schools across the district. Working in pairs, the teachers read several portfolios and assigned ratings, based solely on the documents within the portfolios. These "blind" ratings were then compared with the ratings assigned by the child's own teacher. Discussion usually followed, especially if there were discrepancies or differences in interpretation.

Not all the teachers who were interviewed had attended the meetings, but of those who had, ninety-eight percent stated that these meetings were valuable. Many prefaced their comments with phrases such as, *interesting; an eye opener; very useful; thought it was wonderful; an excellent process.* The reasons they offered in support of these generally favorable evaluations fell into several overlapping categories. These are discussed below.

One of the frequently mentioned benefits of the portfolio scale meetings was in *Building consensus and common language.* Thirty-nine percent of the

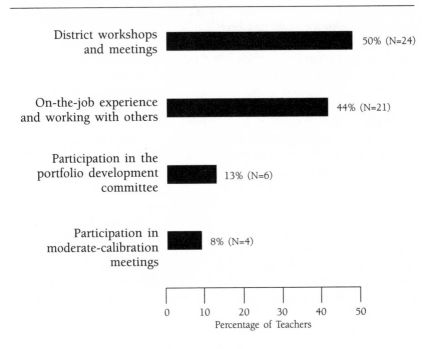

Figure 2: Teachers' Reports of How They Learned to Use the Scale
(based on 48 teachers)

forty-nine responding teachers cited this benefit. A teacher reported that, *you realize we were all thinking the same thing. We're all on the same wave length.* Another teacher stated that the portfolio scale meeting" *was an eye opener because we're isolated* [in different schools]. *You find people who agree with you and have common consensus.* That the meetings were occasions for finding common grounds for assessment of children's reading and writing was a critical aspect for these teachers. They commented on the importance of being on the same wave length, of finding confirmation for their evaluations, and of working through to agreement about the evidence. Others referred explicitly to the value of the process of looking at documents and talking with colleagues. They saw the meetings as beneficial because they served as an opportunity to share perspectives on children's learning and to experience some sense of common language around assessment. A respondent stated, *At first, we were uncomfortable because we did not know the child. As time went on, we both had a better understanding of it* [the scale]. Another stated *It's a great validations and learning process. We had a wide discrepancy on one child. Then we saw that writing was being rated too low.* One teacher also noted the difference between traditional tests as external measures and the scale as a local measure, *Standardized tests give you the grade level, but in the scale we have a language we use and share.*

Thirty-nine percent of the forty-nine responding teachers reported that the portfolio scale meetings *Refined their rating skills.* A teacher stated that the meeting *Helps me to see if I'm going on the right track.* Another reported that *Last year I wasn't as good at scaling as I am now. I got ideas on how to improve the way I scale.* Teachers also talked about "honing" their rating abilities, and of determining whether or not they were "on target." Unlike the first benefit, *Built consensus and common language*, which brought out the qualities of sharing and moderation, the second benefit of *Refined rating skills*, highlights training and the importance of establishing consistent interpretations of the scale. As another teacher stated, *It showed me how I was rating them was the way I should be rating them.* Finally, the refinement was described specifically by a teacher who stated, *It made you take a look at how you rate kids. I think we all went and knocked everybody down a ¹/₂ point.*

Twenty percent of the responding teachers reported that the portfolio scale meetings *Standardized the portfolio procedures.* They drew attention to the meeting's consequences for the teachers' methods of compiling the documents that make up the contents of the portfolio, such as student work samples and teachers' observational records. Several teachers noted that the rating process had brought out the need for greater consistency in data collection so that documents could be reliably read and interpreted. They noted, for example, some differences among teachers in recording reading samples, or selecting writing samples. It also made them appreciate the need, as one stated, *to label and date things for other people.* Comments in this category had brought out the need for greater consistency in data collection so that documents could be reliably read and interpreted. They noted, for example, some differences among teachers in recording reading samples, or selecting writing samples. It also made them appreciate the need, as one stated, *to label and date things for other people.* Comments in this category focused on the portfolio meetings as a quality control strategy to promote consistent and standard practices of portfolio development. The scale itself was not the focus of these remarks; rather, it was the consequent examination of the portfolio's contents, which had been prompted by the use of the scale. Teachers stated, *You see what was in other teacher's folders and what was lacking.* Another stated, *It gets us to get our papers in order.* The need for greater uniformity was echoed in the complaint, *Some teachers did not use the same methods of recording things. There needs to be more consistency.*

In addition to the benefits described above, the comments of 14 percent of the responding teachers suggested that the meetings also *Broadened*

Figure 3: Teachers' Evaluation of the Portfolio Scale Meetings
(based on 49 teachers)

Benefits

Builds consensus and
common language

 39% (N=19)

*"Was an eye opener, because we're isolated. You find people who
 agree with you and have comon consensus."*
*"You could see how kindergarten and first-grade teachers
 looked at and interpreted the same work."*

Refines rating skills

 39% (N=19)

*"We had a wide discrepancy on one. Then we saw that writing was
 being rated too low."*
*"... helps you see if you're being accurate in your assessment of
 the child."*

Standardized portfolio
procedures

 20% (N=10)

*"It makes teachers realize how important it is to label and date
 things for others."*
"You see what was in other teachers' folders and what was lacking."

Broadens understanding of
the rating process

 14% (N=7)

"... if you don't have evidence, you can't rate."
*"You find out if you are really indeed using this material versus
 your [everyday] knowledge."*

Qualifications and Recommendations

 18% (N=9)

*"Wanted to have more time to find out where discrepancies in
 scores existed."*
"The meeting comes too late in the years."

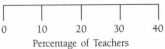

```
0     10     20     30     40
```
Percentage of Teachers

202

understanding of the rating process. These respondents reported that the meetings helped them clarify the distinction between assessment information contained in actual portfolio documents and more informal information that is part of the teachers' personal knowledge of the child. The process of making blind ratings, which was central to the meetings, brought this distinction to the surface. A teacher stated, *You find out if you are really indeed using this material versus your* [everyday] *knowledge about the child.* Another teacher, referring to a discrepancy between her ratings and those of her colleagues conducted *I thought I rated my kids higher than others because I know more about the child.* There were indications that some teachers clearly understood that the scale's scores were to be derived solely from documents of learning in the portfolio and not from general information such as the grade or age of the child. One teacher added, *Interesting that some people ask, "What grade is the child?" This is not an appropriate question when rating.* And concerning portfolios with missing data, a teacher summed it up by stating, *If you don't have evidence, you can't rate.*

Eighteen percent of the responding teachers recommended changes regarding the timing and conduct of the calibration meetings. The *Qualifications and Limitations* expressed by the respondents included feelings that the meetings should occur earlier in the school year, and several wanted more occasions for their portfolios to be read by other teachers. Some also wanted more time in the meetings to discuss and examine score discrepancies. Such criticisms, which were directed at the meeting's procedures, but not its substance, were further evidence that teachers found the meetings worthwhile.

South Brunswick's early literacy portfolio was initially developed in response to teachers' needs for assessment that was in line with classroom practices. The portfolio's developmental scale was constructed in response to administrators' needs to aggregate information for accountability purposes. This study investigates, from the teachers' perspective, the relationship of the developmental scale to their use of the portfolio documents and their evaluation of pupil progress. Analysis of teachers' evaluations of the scale and rating process leads to two major conclusions concerning the scale's consequences for teachers' assessment practices and interpretation of the portfolio.

The numerical scale and rating process do not compete with or replace the teachers' observations and use of portfolio documents as the primary form of evidence.

Teachers' comments concerning both the limitations and benefits of the rating scale indicate that, in their view, the scale is aligned with their own evaluations of student progress. For the most part, the use of the scale appears to confirm what they observe and, occasionally, to provoke a closer examination of the records. Moreover, none of the teachers (not even the few who felt that the scale was not especially useful) complained that the scale's estimates of the children's progress are seriously out of line with their own. The typical concern that elementary teachers raise against the validity of standardized reading tests, that the test results do not match teachers' judgments, are not part of teachers' critique of the scale.

As a corollary, there is little to suggest that the scale has preempted or replaced the portfolio documents and classroom observations as the teachers' primary sources of evidence about pupil learning. While teachers find the scale helpful, they also clearly state that the "real data" are to be found within the portfolio documents, which consist of samples of student work. Although the early literacy portfolio and rating scale have generally replaced test scores and traditional reading readiness assessments as indicators of student progress, the introduction of a scale has *not* resulted in an emphasis on numerical values that overshadow the developmental strategies of literacy development. The teachers do not appear to think of the children's literacy development in numerical terms. This distinction also surfaces in teachers' comments about the portfolio scale meetings when they indicate their belief that the ratings must be grounded in the evidence from the portfolio documents. These remarks, coupled with the finding that the scale is not particularly useful for specific instructional decisions, are further indication that the numerical scale itself plays a supplemental role.

The second conclusion regarding the consequences for teachers' assessment practices and interpretation of the portfolio suggest that: *The scale and rating process serve as a framework for teachers' interpretation of the portfolio and ongoing evaluations of children's early literacy learning.*

The three principal uses of the scale, as reported by teachers, indicate that it provides an assessment framework that is viewed as compatible with the district's curriculum and that articulates for teachers a sense of direction and expectations for learning. That is, the scale is deemed useful for seeing patterns of development, for reviewing and confirming ongoing appraisals, and for communicating with colleagues; it is not reported as being particularly useful for making specific instructional decisions. Such functions suggest that the scale's relationship to classroom practices is an indirect one, mediated by teachers' interpretations and translations. The scale prompts teachers to review information on student progress and to place that information in a developmental context. In that sense, the scale gives the teachers a sense of direction in understanding and evaluating children's progress. However, it does not serve as a diagnostic or prescriptive system. Instead, for their everyday instructional decisions and evaluations, teachers turn to sources of evidence such as student work samples, their own classroom observations, and the actual documents from the portfolio. The scale limitations cited by the teachers are consistent with their statements about the benefits.

In sum, the ratings and scoring system that were designed to meet the district's assessment needs do not appear to undercut the value of the portfolio for meeting teachers' instructional needs. Given the major conclusions of this paper, it appears that the early literacy portfolio scale successfully addresses accountability concerns without detracting from the instructional value of the portfolio documents. In fact, evidence described above indicates that the scale plays a constructive rather than reductive role for teachers.

Appendix References

Baker, E. L., O'Neil, H. F., and Linn, R. L. (1993). Policy and validity prospects for performance-based assessment. *American Psychologist, 48*(12), 1210–18.

Barrs, M., Ellis, S., Hester, H., and Thomas, A. (1989). *Primary language record handbook*. Portsmouth, NH: Heinemann.

Belanoff, P., and Dickson, M. (eds.). (1991). *Portfolios: process and product*. Portsmouth, NH: Heinemann.

Bridgeman, B., Chittenden, E., and Cline, F. (1995). *Characteristics of a portfolio scale for rating early literacy* (Center for Performance Assessment Report no. MS #94–08). Princeton, NJ: Educational Testing Service.

Chittenden, E., and Spicer, W. (1993). *The South Brunswick literacy portfolio project*. Paper presented at the New Standards Project: English Language arts Portfolio Meeting, Minneapolis, MN.

Clay, M. M. (1985). *The early detection of reading* (3rd ed.). Aukland, New Zealand: Heinemann.

Holdaway, D. (1979). *The Foundations of Literacy*. New York: Ashton Scholastic.

LeMahieu, P. G., Eresh, J. T., & Wallace, R. C. (1992). Using student portfolios for a public accounting. *School Administrator, 49*(11), 8–15.

Mitchell, R. (1992). *Testing for learning: How new approaches to evaluation can improve American schools*. New York: Free Press.

Murphy, S. (1994). Portfolios and curriculum reform: Patterns in practice. *Assessing Writing, 1*(2), 175–206.

Valencia, S. W., and Calfee, R. (1991). The development and use of literacy portfolios for students, classes, and teachers. *Applied Measurement in Education, 4*(4), 333–45.

Wiggins, G. (1993). *Assessing student performance: Exploring the purpose and limits of testing*. San Francisco: Jossey-Bass.

Supplement Appendix

South Brunswick Early Literacy Portfolio Scale

South Brunswick Literacy Portfolio Scale
K–2 South Brunswick School District Reading/Writing Scale (Draft 5)
Development of Children's Strategies for Making Sense of Print

Level 1: EARLY EMERGENT
Displays an awareness of some conventions of reading, such as front/back of books, distinctions between print and pictures. Sees the construction of meaning from text as "magical" or exterior to the print. While the child may be interested in the contents of books, there is as yet little apparent attention to turning written marks into language. Is beginning to notice environmental print.

Level 2: ADVANCED EMERGENT
Engages in pretend reading and writing. Uses readinglike ways that clearly approximate book language. Demonstrates a sense of the story being "read," using picture clues and recall of story line. May draw upon predictable language patterns in anticipating (and recalling) the story. Attempts to use letters in writing, sometimes in random or scribble fashion.

Level 3: EARLY BEGINNING READER
Attempts to "really read." Indicates beginning sense of one-to-one correspondence and concept of word. Predicts actively in new material, using syntax and story line. Small stable sight vocabulary is becoming established. Evidence of initial awareness of beginning and ending sounds, especially in invented spelling.

Level 4: ADVANCED BEGINNING READER
Starts to draw on major cue systems; self-corrects or identifies words through use of letter-sound patterns, sense of story, or syntax. Reading may be laborious especially with new material, requiring considerable effort and some support. Writing and spelling reveal awareness of letter patterns and conventions of writing such as capitalization and periods.

Level 5: EARLY INDEPENDENT READER
Handles familiar material on own, but still needs some support with unfamiliar material. Figures out words and self-corrects by drawing on a combination of letter-sound relationships, word structure, story line, and syntax. Strategies of rereading or of guessing from larger chunks of texts are becoming well established. Has a large stable sight vocabulary. Conventions of writing are understood.

Level 6: ADVANCED INDEPENDENT READER

Reads independently, using multiple strategies flexibly. Monitors and self-corrects for meaning. Can read and understand most material when the content is appropriate. Conventions of writing and spelling are—for the most part—under control.

Note 1: The scale focuses on development of children's strategies for making sense of print. Evidence concerning children's strategies and knowledge about print may be revealed in both their reading and writing activities.

Note 2: The scale does not attempt to rate children's interests or attitudes regarding reading, nor does it attempt to summarize what literature may mean to the child. Such aspects of children's literacy development are summarized in other forms.

Rating scale developed by South Brunswick teachers and ETS staff—January 1991

A Three-Stage Model of Mathematics and Science Development in Young Children[*]

Stage 1—Preschool 3 and 4
Mathematical Thinking

Description of Stage I

At Stage I the child shows curiosity about and interest in numbers, counting, the mechanics of numbers and quantity, and may ask questions in this regard. Also at Stage I, the child can reproduce a simple pattern of two or three parts either visually or auditorily, and is able to group objects that vary according to only one attribute such as color, size, or shape. Simple comparisons between groups or between single objects are made. The child may arrange two or three objects according to one attribute such as big and little, long and short. At Stage I the child is able to make one-to-one correspondence with up to five objects. The child is also able to demonstrate awareness of "more than" or "less than" when objects are added or removed from a set. Several shapes may be identified and described.

Language consists of propositional words such as *top, bottom, up, down, in, out, above, below, under, beside, behind*. General terms, such as *big and small*, are used to describe people and objects. At Stage I the child participates in activities such as cooking, paint mixing, and charting temperature

---

[*]Adapted for *The Work Sampling System,* 1992–93 Field Trial Edition, Marsden, Meisels, and Jablon. Education Testing Service, 1993. Reprinted by permission of Educational Testing Service, the copyright owner.

changes. Reference to time are primarily in the present such as, "It's sleepy time."

The child at Stage I also expresses an interest in, explores, and asks questions about the natural and physical world. Similarities and differences are observed. The child expresses curiosity about scientific investigations by proposing explanations and experiments with materials to discover "what would happen if."

Approaches to Mathematical Thinking

(1) not yet evident; (2) emergent; (3) strongly evident

Shows curiosity about and interest in numbers, counting, and quality		1	2	3
	Fall			
	Winter			
	Spring			

Wants to learn the mechanics of numbers and numerals; asks questions				
	Fall			
	Winter			
	Spring			

Patterns and Classification

Reproduces visually or auditorily a simple pattern of two or three parts				
	Fall			
	Winter			
	Spring			

Patterns and Classification (*continued*)

(1) not yet evident; (2) emergent; (3) strongly evident

Groups objects that vary according to only one attribute		1	2	3
	Fall			
	Winter			
	Spring			

Identifies simple two- or three-part patterns either visually or auditorily				
	Fall			
	Winter			
	Spring			

Sorts objects into groups according to a single attribute, such as color, size, or shape				
	Fall			
	Winter			
	Spring			

Makes comparisons between groups or between single objects				
	Fall			
	Winter			
	Spring			

	1	2	3
Fall			
Winter			
Spring			

Arranges two or three objects in order on the basis of one attribute such as size (e.g., big and little, long and short, etc.)

Number Concept

	1	2	3
Fall			
Winter			
Spring			

Makes one-to-one correspondence with up to five objects

	1	2	3
Fall			
Winter			
Spring			

Verbalizes "more than" when objects are added to a set and "less than" when objects are removed from a set

Geometry and Spatial Relationships

(1) not yet evident; (2) emergent; (3) strongly evident

	1	2	3
Identifies and describes several shapes	Fall		
	Winter		
	Spring		

Uses positional words (e.g., top, bottom, up, down, in, above, below, under, beside, behind)	Fall		
	Winter		
	Spring		

Measurement

Uses the general terms "big," "small," "heavy," "bigger," "smaller," and "heavier" appropriately to describe people and objects	Fall		
	Winter		
	Spring		

	1	2	3
Fall			
Winter			
Spring			

Uses nonstandard units of measurement to estimate size and weight

Fall			
Winter			
Spring			

Participates in measuring activities such as cooking, paint mixing, and charting temperature changes

Fall			
Winter			
Spring			

Refers to time primarily in the present or in terms of events (e.g., "it's sleepy time," or an hour is as long as "one Sesame Street")

215

Scientific Thinking

(1) not yet evident; (2) emergent; (3) strongly evident

Observation

	1	2	3
Expresses an interest in and explores toys, sand, water, sound, tools, and simple machines — Fall			
Winter			
Spring			

	1	2	3
Make comparisons about what has been observed, and finds similarities and differences — Fall			
Winter			
Spring			

*Adapted for *The Work Sampling System*, 1992–93 Field Trial Edition, Marsden, Meisels, and Jablon. Education Testing Service, 1993.

Questioning, Predicting and Explaining

	1	2	3
Asks questions about the natural and physical world while exploring the objects and interest areas set up in the classroom	Fall		
	Winter		
	Spring		

Expresses curiosity about scientific investigation by proposing explanations	Fall		
	Winter		
	Spring		

Experiments with materials to find out "what would happen if"	Fall		
	Winter		
	Spring		

217

Appendix B

Stage II—K/1
Mathematical Thinking

Description of Stage II

At Stage II the child shows curiosity in solving mathematical problems by relating previous information to new knowledge, beginning to draw logical conclusions from information already acquired, and beginning to develop and use strategies for solving problems.

Language is used to describe mathematical ideas and mathematical thinking is communicated by explaining an idea. Propositional words such as *above, below, to, from, low* and *high* are used to express relationships, terms such as *few and many, empty and full* are used appropriately.

The child sees, extends, and duplicates patterns and relationships and can create her or his own pattern with actions, words, and objects. The child is also able to sort objects into subgroups and classifies them according to a rule such as color, size, and things to eat. Comparisons between subgroups are also made such as "all of these blocks are red," "some of these stick are short." A variety of materials and objects can be sorted on the basis of a number of attributes such as size, length, volume, and quantity. The child shows an understanding of the concept of number and quantity, demonstrates an understanding of relationships between quantities, and makes reasonable estimates of quantities. A variety of shapes can be identified, relationships between shapes are recognized, and three-dimensional models can be constructed from models.

At Stage II the child can estimate and measure length, weight, and capacity using nonstandard units. The child demonstrates an emerging understanding of time and uses time-related words in daily vocabulary.

At Stage II the child collects data and records information using tallies, lists, or graphs. The child is able to read and draw conclusions from a simple graph. Simple predictions are made based on experience. In general, the child also describes and distinguishes between living and nonliving things, poses questions, makes predictions, and proposes explanations based on experience.

Adapted for *The Work Sampling System*, 1992–93 Field Trial Edition, Marsden, Meisels, and Jablon. Educational Testing Service, 1993.

Approaches to Mathematical Thinking

(1) not yet evident; (2) emergent; (3) strongly evident

1.

	1	2	3
Relates previous information to new knowledge; begins to draw logical conclusions from information already acquired; and begins to develop and use strategies for solving problems			
Fall			
Winter			
Spring			

2.

Uses words to describe mathematical ideas			
Fall			
Winter			
Spring			

219

Approaches to Mathematical Thinking *(continued)*

(1) not yet evident; (2) emergent; (3) strongly evident

3.

	1	2	3
Communicates mathematical thinking by explaining an idea			
Fall			
Winter			
Spring			

Patterns and Relationships

1.

Sees a pattern and can extend or duplicate it; can create own pattern with actions, words, and objects			
Fall			
Winter			
Spring			

2.

Sorts objects into subgroups and classifies the subgroups according to a rule (e.g., color, size, things to eat, shape, and texture)			
Fall			
Winter			
Spring			

3.

	1	2	3
Makes comparisons between subgroups using words like "all" and "some" (e.g., all of these blocks are red, some of these sticks are short)			
Fall			
Winter			
Spring			

4.

Orders a variety of materials or objects on the basis of a number of attributes such as size (large to small), length (short to long), volume of sounds (loud to soft), and quantity			
Fall			
Winter			
Spring			

Number Concepts

(1) not yet evident; (2) emergent; (3) strongly evident

1.

Makes one-to-one correspondence with five to ten objects	1	2	3
Fall			
Winter			
Spring			

2.

Shows understanding of relationships between quantities (e.g., knows when a quantity is less than a certain number or when one group has more than another group)	1	2	3
Fall			
Winter			
Spring			

3.

Models, reads, writes, and compares whole numbers up to 20	1	2	3
Fall			
Winter			
Spring			

4.

Counts (up to 20) objects in a group using one-to-one correspondence		1	2	3
	Fall			
	Winter			
	Spring			

5.

Uses counting strategies, e.g., "counting on," "counting backward," or counting in groups (e.g., 2, 5, 10)				
	Fall			
	Winter			
	Spring			

6.

Makes reasonable estimates of quantities				
	Fall			
	Winter			
	Spring			

Number Concepts *(continued)*

(1) not yet evident; (2) emergent; (3) strongly evident

8.

		1	2	3
Uses strategies to add and substract numbers to 10	Fall			
	Winter			
	Spring			

9.

		1	2	3
Shows beginning understanding of place value	Fall			
	Winter			
	Spring			

Geometry and Spatial Relationships

1.

		1	2	3
Identifies, labels, and draws a variety of shapes	Fall			
	Winter			
	Spring			

2.

Uses potitional words to express relaionships (e.g., above, below, to, from, low, high, inside, outside, behind, far, near, to the left or right)

	1	2	3
Fall			
Winter			
Spring			

3.

Constructs three-dimensional forms from models

Fall			
Winter			
Spring			

4.

Recognizes shapes and the relationships between shapes while exploring puzzles and manipulatives

Fall			
Winter			
Spring			

Geometry and Spatial Relationships *(continued)*

5.

(1) not yet evident; (2) emergent; (3) strongly evident

	1	2	3
Recognizes some of the properties of two- and three-dimensional structures	Fall		
	Winter		
	Spring		

Measurement

1.

	1	2	3
Uses and understands such terms as "few and many," "empty and full," and "longer and shorter"	Fall		
	Winter		
	Spring		

2.

Estimates and measures length, weight, and capacity informally, using nonstandard units		1	2	3
	Fall			
	Winter			
	Spring			

3.

Shows an interest in and explores common instruments for measuring (e.g., scales for weight, cup for volume, thermometer for temperature)				
	Fall			
	Winter			
	Spring			

4.

Shows a beginning understanding of time and describes the sequence of activities in a regular schedule using such words as "today" "yesterday"; compares time to known events				
	Fall			
	Winter			
	Spring			

227

Measurement (*continued*)

(1) not yet evident; (2) emergent; (3) strongly evident

5.

		1	2	3
Uses time-related words in daily vocabulary (e.g., day, week, month, year) with relative accuracy and tells time to the nearest hour	Fall			
	Winter			
	Spring			

6.

Identifies different coins	Fall			
	Winter			
	Spring			

Probability and Statistics

1.

Collects and records data using tallies, lists, and charts; makes and uses "real graphs" (using actual objects) and simple picture graphs	Fall			
	Winter			
	Spring			

2.

Reads a simple graph or chart and draws conclusions from it		1	2	3
	Fall			
	Winter			
	Spring			

3.

Makes simple predictions based on experience				
	Fall			
	Winter			
	Spring			

Scientific Thinking

(1) not yet evident; (2) emergent; (3) strongly evident

Observation

1.

Uses senses to observe the characteristics or behaviors of living and nonliving things		1	2	3
	Fall			
	Winter			
	Spring			

2.

Describes and classifies living and nonliving things in different ways				
	Fall			
	Winter			
	Spring			

3.

Makes comparisons based on observations; finds similarities and differences				
	Fall			
	Winter			
	Spring			

Questioning, Predicting, and Explaining

1.

Expresses a sense of wonder by asking questions and making predictions about the natural and physical world		1	2	3
	Fall			
	Winter			
	Spring			

2.

Seeks out answers to questions through active exploration, looking in books, and asking others				
	Fall			
	Winter			
	Spring			

3.

Proposes explanations based on observations				
	Fall			
	Winter			
	Spring			

231

Questioning, Predicting, and Explaining *(continued)*

(1) not yet evident; (2) emergent; (3) strongly evident

4.

	1	2	3
Draws conclusions based on observation and experimentation	Fall		
	Winter		
	Spring		

Describing and Communicating Findings

1.

Uses descriptive language to communicate observations and experimentation	Fall		
	Winter		
	Spring		

2.

Uses drawings to record findings and writes simple one-word or one-sentence captions	Fall		
	Winter		
	Spring		

Stage III—2/3
Mathematical Thinking

Description of Stage III

At Stage III the child explores and classifies shapes, recognizes specific attributes, and solves spatial problems by manipulating objects and by drawing. The child demonstrates an understanding of coins and bills. Estimates and measurements are done with nonstandard measures, but words are used appropriately to describe and compare measurements. Time-related words such as day, week, and month are used in daily vocabulary. Descriptive language is used to communicate observations and experimentation.

At Stage III the child can collect and record data and can make, read, and interpret graphs. Predictions based on her or his own experience can be made. The child makes comparisons based on observations of living versus nonliving things. A hallmark of this stage is the child's search for answers to questions through *active* investigation and the ability to draw conclusions based on observation and experimentation.

---

*Adapted for *The Work Sampling System,* 1992–93 Field Trial Edition, Marsden, Meisels, and Jablon. Educational Testing Service, 1993.

To Mathematical Thinking

(1) not yet evident; (2) emergent; (3) strongly evident

1.

Explores and classifies shapes, recognizing specific attributes	1	2	3
Fall			
Winter			
Spring			

2.

Solves spatial problems using manipulatives and drawings			
Fall			
Winter			
Spring			

3.

Explores properties of two- and three-dimensional constructions			
Fall			
Winter			
Spring			

4.

Shows understanding of coins and bills			
Fall			
Winter			
Spring			

234

Measurement

1.

	Fall	Winter	Spring
	1	2	3

Estimates and measures using nonstandard and standard units; uses words to describe and compare measurements

	1	2	3
Fall			
Winter			
Spring			

2.

Shows interest in and explores common instruments for measuring (e.g., scales for weight, cups for volume, thermometer)

	1	2	3
Fall			
Winter			
Spring			

3.

Uses time-related words in a daily vocabulary (e.g., day, week, month, year) with accuracy; can read time on the clock

	1	2	3
Fall			
Winter			
Spring			

235

Probability and Statistics

(1) not yet evident; (2) emergent; (3) strongly evident

1.

	1	2	3
Collects and records data using tallies, lists, and charts; makes and uses graphs to display data — Fall			
Winter			
Spring			

2.

Reads graphs or charts and draws conclusions from them — Fall			
Winter			
Spring			

3.

Makes predictions based on experience — Fall			
Winter			
Spring			

236

Stage III: Elementary Education 2/3
Scientific Thinking

(1) not yet evident; (2) emergent; (3) strongly evident

Observation

1.

		1	2	3
Describes, classifies, and categorizes living and nonliving things in different ways	Fall			
	Winter			
	Spring			

2.

		1	2	3
Makes comparisons based on observations	Fall			
	Winter			
	Spring			

237

Questioning, Predicting, and Explaining

(1) not yet evident; (2) emergent; (3) strongly evident

1.

		1	2	3
Expresses a sense of wonder by asking questions and making predictions about the natural and physical world	Fall			
	Winter			
	Spring			

2.

Seeks out answers to questions by active investigation	Fall			
	Winter			
	Spring			

3.

Draws conclusions based on observation and experimentation	Fall			
	Winter			
	Spring			

238

Describing and Communicating Findings

1.

		1	2	3
Uses descriptive language to communicate observations and experimentation	Fall			
	Winter			
	Spring			

2.

Records findings using drawings, graphs, and written descriptions	Fall			
	Winter			
	Spring			

239

Comments

REFERENCES

Advocates for Children (1992). *Segregated and second rate: Special education in New York*. New York, NY.

Alberto, P. A., and Troutman, A. C. (1995). *Applied behavior analysis for teachers* (4th ed.). Columbus, OH: Chas E. Merrill.

Algozzine, B., Christenson, S., and Ysseldyke, J. (1982). Probabilities associated with the referral to placement process. *Teacher Education and Special Education, 5,* 19–23.

Alley, G., and Deshler, D. (1979). *Teaching the learning disabled adolescent: Strategies and methods*. Denver: Love Publishing.

Anderson, P. L., Cronin, M. E., and Miller, J. H. (1986). Referral reasons for learning disabled students. *Psychology in the Schools, 23,* 388–95.

Anderson-Inman, L. (1986). Bridging the gap: Student-generated strategies for promoting the transfer of learning. *Exceptional Children, 52,* 562–72.

Bahr, M., Fuchs D., Strecker, P., Goodman, B., and Fuchs, L. (1988). *Characteristics of students targeted for prereferral intervention*. Paper presented at the annual meeting of the National Association of School Psychologists, Chicago.

Bay, M., and Bryan, T. (1992). Differentiating children who are at risk for referral from others: A critical classroom factors *Remedial and Special Education, 13* 27–33.

Bigge, J. (1988) *Curriculum based instruction for special education*. Columbus, Ohio: Mayfield.

Bos, C. S., and Vaughan, S. (1994). *Strategies for teaching students with learning and behavior problems* (3rd ed.). Boston: Allyn & Bacon.

Brophy, J., and Good, T. (1974). *Teacher-student relationships: Causes and consequences*. New York: Holt, Rinehart, and Winston.

Brown A. L., and Campione, J. C. (1986). Psychological theory and the study of learning disabilities. *American Psychologist, 14* (10), 1059–68.

241

Brown, R., and Elliot, R. (1965). Control of aggression in a nursery school class. *Journal of Experimental Child Psychology, 2,* 103–7.

Bucher, B., and King, L. W. (1971). Generalization punishment effect in the deviant behavior of psychotic child. *Behavior Therapy, 2,* 68–71.

Bushell, D. (1973) The behavior analysis classroom. In B. Spoked (ed.), *Early Childhood Education.* Englewood Cliffs, NJ: Prentice-Hall.

Camp, R. (1992). Assessment in the context of schools and school change. In H. H. Marshall (ed.), *Redefining student learning: Roots of educational change.* Norwood, NJ: Ablex, 241–263.

Calkins, L. Mc.C. (1986). *The art of teaching writing.* Portsmouth, NH: Heinemann.

Carter, J., and Sugai, G. (1989). Survey on preferral practices: Responses from state departments of education. *Exceptional Children, 55,* 298–302.

Cartledge, G., and Milburn, J. F. (eds.). (1980). *Teaching social skills to children.* New York: Pergamon.

Cartledge, G., Lee, J. W., and Feng, H. (1995). Cultural diversity: Multicultural factors in teaching social skills. In C. Cartledge and J. F. Milburn, (eds.), *Teaching social skills to children and youth* (pp. 328–55). Boston: Allyn & Bacon.

Chalfant, J. C., and Pysh, M. V. (1989). Teacher assistance teams: Five descriptive studies on 96 teams. *Remedial and Special Education, 10* (6), 298–302.

Chalfant, J. C., Pysh, M. V. D., and Moultrie, R. (1997). Teacher assistance teams: A model for within building problem solving. *Learning Disability Quarterly, 2,* 85–96.

Chinn, P. C., and Hughes, S. (1987). Representation of minority students in special education classes. *Remedial and Special Education, 8* (4) 4–46.

Chittenden, T. (1991). Authentic assessment, evaluation, and documentation of student performance. In V. Perrone (ed.), *Expanding student assessment* (pp. 23–31). Alexandria, VA: Association for Supervision and Curriculum Development.

Choate, J. S. and Evans, S. S. (1992). Authentic assessment of special learners: Problem or Provise. *Parenting School Failure, 27,* 1, 6–9.

Choate, J. S., Bennett, T. Z., Enright, B. E., Miller, L. J., Poteet, J. A., and Raker, T. A. (1987). *Assessing and programming basic curriculum skills.* Boston: Allyn & Bacon.

Collier, J. (1988). Sociocultural considerations when referring minority children for learning disabilities. *Learning Disabilities Focus, 31,* 39–43.

Commission on Special Education (1985). *Special Eduation: A call for quality.* New York, NY.

Davidman, L., and Davidman, P. T. (1994). *Teaching with a multicultural perspective. A practical guide.* White Plains, NY: Longman Publishing Group.

Deno, S., and Merkin, P. (1997). *Data-based program modification*. Reston, VA: C.E.C. Publications.

Dent, H. (1994). Testing African American children: The struggle continues. *Psych Discourse, 25,* 5–9.

Deshler, D. D., Ellis, E. S., and Lenz, B. K. (1996). *Teaching adolescents with learning disabilities: Strategies and methods* (2nd ed.). Denver: Love Publishing Co.

Deshler, D., and Schumacher, J. B. (1986). Learning strategies: An instructional alternative for low achieving adolescents. *Exceptional Children, 52,* 583–89.

Drabman, R. S., and Lahey, B. B. (1974). Feedback in classroom behavior modification: Effects on the target and her classmates. *Journal of Applied Behavior Analysis, 7,* 591–98.

Falk, B., and Darling-Hammond, L. (1992). The primary language record at P.S. 261: How assessment transforms teaching and learning. Unpublished case study, National Center for Restructuring Education, Schools, and Teaching, Columbia University.

Ferritor, D. E., Buchholdt, D., Hamblin, R. L., and Smith, L. (1972). The non-effects of contingency reinforcement of attending behavior on work accomplished. *Journal of Applied Behavior Analysis, 5,* 7–17.

Ford, A. F. (1992). Multicultural education training for special educators working with African American Youths. *Exceptional Children, 59,* 107–14.

Foster, G. G., Ysseldyke, J. E., Casey, A., and Thurlow, M. L. (1974). the congruence between reason for referral and placement outcome. *Journal of Psychoeducational Assessment, 2,* 209–17.

Fradd, S., and Hallman, C. L. (1983). Implications of psychological and educational research for assessment and instruction of culturally linguistically different students. *Learning Disability Quarterly, 6,* 468–78.

Fradd, S. H., and Weismantel, M. J. (1989). Developing and evaluating goals. In S. H. Fradd and M. J. Weismantel (eds.), *Meeting the needs of culturally and linguistically different students: A handouts for educators* (pp. 34–64). Boston: College Hill.

Friend, M., and McNutt, M. G. (1984). Resource room programs: Where are we now? *Exceptional Children, 51,* 150–55.

Fuchs, D., and Fuchs, L. (1994). Reintegration of students with learning disabilities into the mainstream: A two-year study. Paper presented at the Annual Convention of the C.E.C. Denver, April 6–10.

Galagan, J. E. (1985). Psychoeducational testing: Turnout the lights, the party's over. *Exceptional Children, 52* (3), 288–99.

Garcia, S. B., and Ortiz, A. A. (1988). *Preventing inappropriate referrals of language minority students to special education*. Wheaton, MD: National Clearinghouse for Bilingual Education.

Gardner, H. (1983). *Frames of mind: The theory of multiple intelligence.* New York: Basic Books.

Gearheart, B. R. (1985). *Learning disabilities: Educational strategies* (4th ed.). St. Louis: Times/Mirror/Mosby College Publications.

Glatthorn, A. A. (1990). Cooperative professional development: A tested approach not a panacea. *RASE, 11,* 4, 62.

Goldstein, A. P., Sprafkin, R. P., Gershaw, N. J., and Klein, P. (1980). *Skillstreaming the adolescent: A structural learning approach to teaching prosocial skills.* Champaign, IL: Research Press.

Gottlieb, J., Gottlieb, B. W., and Trogone, S. (1991). Parent and teacher referrals for psychoeducational evaluation. *Journal of Special Education, 25,* 155–67.

Graden, J. L., Casey, A., and Chistenson, S. L. (1985). Implementing a preferral intervention system: Part I. The model. *Exceptional Children, 51,* 5, 377–83.

Graham, S., and Miller, L. (1979). Spelling research and practice: A unified approach. *Focus on Exceptional Children.*

———. *(1980).* Handwriting remediation and principles: A unified approach. *Focus on Exceptional Children, 12,* 2.

Graves, D. H. (1983) *Writing: Teachers and children at work.* Portsmouth, NH: Heinemann.

Greer, R. D., and Dorow, L. G. (1976). *Specializing educational behaviorally: A data-based approach for teachers in special education.* Dubuque, Iowa: Kendall/Hunt.

Grossman, H. (1996). *Special education in a diverse society.* Boston: Allyn & Bacon.

———. (1992). *The San Jose State University Bilingual/Multicultural Special Education Personnel Preparations Program: A report on thirteen years of experience.* San Jose, CA: San Jose State University (ERIC Document no. 364–092).

Hall, R. V. (1971). *Managing behavior.* Lawrence, KS: H & H Enterprises.

Hall, R. V., Fox, R., Willard, D., Goldsmith, L., Emerson, M., Owen, M., Davis, F., and Procia, F. (1971). The teacher as observer and experimenter in the modification of disputing and talking out behavior. *Journal of applied Behavior Analysis, 4,* 141–49.

Hanser, S. B. (1973). *Group contingent music listening in emotionally disturbed boys.* Paper presented to the twenty-fourth annual convention of the National Association for Music Therapy, Athens, GA.

Harris, F. R., Johnson, M., Kelly, C. S., and Wolf, M. M. (1966). Effects of positive social reinforcement on regressed crawling of a nursery school child. *Journal of Educational Psychology, 55,* 35–41.

Harry, B. (1992). These families, those families: The import of research identities on the research art. *Exceptional Children, 62* (4), 292–300.

Harry, B., Allen, N., and McLaughlin, M. (1995). Communication versus compliance: African-American parents' involvement in special education. *Exceptional Children, 61,* 364–77.

Hawkins, R. P., Peterson, R. K., Schweid, E., and Bijou, S. (1966). Behavior therapy in the home: Ameiloration of problem parent-child relations with the parent in a therapeutic role. *Journal of Experimental Child Psychology, 4,* 99–77.

Hearne, D., and Stone, S. (1995). Multiple intelligencies and underachievement: Lessons for individuals with learning disabilities. *Journal of Learning Disabilities, 28* (7), 439, 448.

Henry, N. A., and Flynn, E. S. (1990) Rethinking special education referral: A procedural manual. *Intervention in School and Clinic, 26,* 22–24.

Hill, M. (1992). *Training African-American parents for success: An Afrocentric parenting guide.* Cleveland, OH: East End Neighborhood House.

Hilliard, A. (1987). (ed.). *The Negro Educational Review, 38* (2–3) Entire issue.

Holmes, D. S. (1996). The application of learning theory in the treatment of a school behavior problem: A case study. *Psychology in the Schools, 3,* 355–58.

Homme, C. (1970). *How to use contingency contracts in the classroom.* Champaign, IL: Research Press.

Hoover, J. J., and Collier, C. (1992). Sociocultural considerations in teaching study strategies. *Intervention in School and Clinic. 27,* 4, 228–32.

Hopkins, B. L., and Conard, R. V. (1976). Putting it all together: Super school. In N. Haring and R. Shiefelbush, *Teaching exceptional children.* New York: McGraw-Hill.

Howe, K. R., and Miramantes, O. B. (1992). *The ethics of special education.* New York: Teachers College Press.

Howell, K. W., and Morehead, M. K. (1987). *Curriculum-based evaluation for special and remedial education.* Columbus, Ohio: Merrill.

Hudson, F. G., and Graham, S. (1978). An approach to operationalizing the IEP. *Learning Disabilities Quarterly, 1,* 13–32.

Isaacson, S. (1988). Teaching written expression. *Teaching Exceptional Children, 20,* 32–22.

Johnson, D. W., and Johnson, R. T. (1994). *Learning together and alone: Cooperative, competitive and individualized learning* (4th ed.). Boston: Allyn & Bacon.

———. (1996). Peacemakers: Teaching students to resolve their own schoolmates' conflicts. In E. L. Meyer, G. A. Vergason, and R. J. Whelan (eds.), *Strategies for teaching exceptional children in inclusive settings* (pp. 311–28). Denver: Love Publishing Co.

Johnson, D. J., and Mylkebust, H. R. (1967). Learning disabilities: Educational principles and practices. New York: Gurne and Stratton.

Johnson, L. J., Pugach, M. C., and Hammittee, D. (1988). Bariers to effective special education consultation. *Remedial and Special Education, 9,* 41–47.

Jones, J., and Chittenden, T. (1995). *Teachers' perception of rating an early literacy portfolio.* Princeton, NJ: Educational Testing Service.

Jones, R. L. (ed.). (1988). *Psychoeducational assessment of minority group children: A casebook.* Berkeley, CA: Cobb & Henry Publishers.

Jones, R. L. (ed.). (1991). *Black psychology* (3rd ed.). Berkeley: Cobb and Henry.

Kalyanpur, M., and Rao, S. (1991). Empowering low-income, black families of handicapped children. *American Journal of Orthopsychiatry, 61,* (4), 523–32.

Kazdin, A. E. (1973). The effects of vicarious reinforcement of attending behavior in classroom. *Journal of Applied Behavior Analysis, 6,* 71–78.

Kirk, S., and Chalfant, J. (1984). *Academic and Developmental Learning Disabilities,* Denver: Love.

Koegal, R. L., and Covert, A. (1972). The relationship of self-stimulation to learning in autistic children. *Journal of Applied Behavior Analysis, 5,* 381–87.

Kroth, R. L. (1985). *Communicating with parents of exceptional children* (2nd ed.). Denver: Love Publishing.

Kroth, R. L., and Simpson, R. L. (1977). *Parent conferences as a teaching strategy.* Denver: Love Publishing.

Kruger, L. J., Struzziero, Watts, R., and Vocca, D. (1995). The relationship between organizational support and satisfaction with teacher assistance teams. *RASE, 16,* 4, 203–11.

Lerner, J. (1993). *Learning disabilities: Theories, diagnosis and teaching strategies* (6th ed.). Boston: Houghton Mufflin Co.

Leung, B. (1996). Quality assessment priorities in a diverse society. *Teaching Exceptional Children,* spring, 42–45.

Lochner, P. A., and McNamara, B. E. (1989). Meeting the needs of the atypical learner. Paper presented at the annual convention of the C.E.C. Toronto, April.

Lyman, L., Foyle, H. C., and Azwell, T. S. (1993). Cooperative learning in the elementary classroom. Washington, D.C.: NEA Professional Library.

Maheady, L., Towne, R., Algozzine, B., Mercer, J., and Ysseldyke, J. (1983). Minority overpresentation: A case for alternative practices prior to referral. *Learning Disabilities Quarterly, 64,* 448–56.

Maher, C. A., and Bennett, R. E. (1984). *Planning and evaluating special education services.* Englewood Cliffs, NJ: Prentice-Hall.

Maher, C. A., and Illback, R. J. (1985). Implementing school psychological programs: Description and application of the DURABLE approach. *Journal of School Psychology,* Springfield, IL: Charles C. Thomas.

Manning, M. L., and Barnth, L. G. (1996). *Multicultural education of children and adolecesents*. Boston: Allyn & Bacon.

Margolis, H., and Brannigan, G. G. (1986). Building trust with parents. *Academic Therapy, 22, 1,* 71–74.

Marrapoli, Guzman M. (1992). *Success for each child: A research-based report on eliminating tracking in New York City public schools.* The Fund for New York City Public Education, New York, NY.

McDaniel, T. R. (1986). A primer on classroom discipline: Principles old and new. *Phi Delta Kappa,* Sept., 63–67.

McNamara, B. E. (1977). *The effects of instruction in principals of learning and techniques of teaching versus techniques of teaching on teachers' social reinforcement behavior.* Doctoral dissertation, Teachers College, Columbia University.

———. (1979). Talk without "teacherses." *Academic Therapy, 15,* 227–30.

———. (1986). Parents as parents in the I.E.P. process. *Academic Therapy, 21,* 309–19.

———. (1989). *The resource room. A guide for special educators.* Albany, NY: State University of New York Press.

McNamara, B. E., and McNamara, F. J. (1995). *Keys to parenting a child with a learning disability.* Hauppauge, NY: Barrons Educational Services.

Madsen, C. K., and Forsythe, L. J. (1974). The effect of contingent music on increases of mathematical responses. In C. K. Madsen, R. D. Greer, and C. H. Madsen (eds.), *Research in music behavior.* New York: Teachers College Press.

Madsen, C. K., and Madsen (1974). *Teaching/discipline: A positive approach for educational development* (3rd ed.). Boston: Allyn & ampersand Bacon.

Mercer, C. D., and Mercer, A. R. (1996). *Teaching students with learning problems* (4th ed.). Columbus, OH: Chas. E. Merrill.

Mercer, J. (1983). Issues in the diagnosis of language disorders in students whose primarily language is not English. *Journal of Speech and Hearing Research, 16,* 642–49.

Messick, S. (1987). *Assessment in the schools: Purposes and consequences* (Research Report RR-87-51): Educational Testing Service, Princeton, NJ.

Michaels, S. (1989). *The Literacies Institute: Its mission, activities, and perspective on literacy* (1): Literacies Institute.

Murray, D. M. (1982). *Living by teaching.* Upper Montclair, NJ: Boynton/Cook Publishers.

Myers, P., and Hammill, D. D. (1976). *Methods for learning disorders* (2nd ed.). New York: John Wiley.

Nuttall, E. V., Landurand, P., M., and Goldman, P. (1984). A critical look at testing and evaluation from a cross-cultural perspective. In P. C. Chinn (ed.), *Education of culturally and linguistically different children.* Reston, VA: Council for Exceptional Children.

Ogbu, J. V. (1992). Understanding cultural diversity and learning. *Educational Research, 21,* (8), 14–24.

O'Leary, S. G., and O'Leary, K. D. (1976). Behavior modification in the school. In H. Leitenberg (ed.), *Handbook of behavior modification.* Englewood Cliffs, NJ: Prentice Hall.

Palincsar, A. S. (1986). Metacognitive strategy instruction. *Exceptional Children, 53,* 118–24.

Parsonson, B., Baer, A., and Baer, D. (1974). The application of generalized correct social contingencies: An evaluation of training program. *Journal of Applied Behavior Analysis, 7,* 427–37.

Peenan, J. (1995). Danger signs of overrepresentation of minorities in special education. *C.E.C. Today.* September, p. 7.

Perl, J. Improving relationship skills for parent conferences (1995). *Teaching Exceptional Children,* (1995), *28,* (1) 29–31.

Picone-Zocchia, J. (1997). Portfolios prompt sheets. West Islip Central School District, West Islip, New York.

Pike, K., and Solend, S. J. (1995). Authentic assessment strategies. Alternative to norm-referenced testing. *Teaching Exceptional Children,* (1995), *28* (1), 15–21.

Plata, M. (1983). Using Spanish-speaking interpreters in special education. *Remedial and Special Education, 14,* 5, 19–23.

Plata, M. (1993) Using Spanish-speaking interpreters in special education. *Remedial Special Education, 14,* (5), 19–23.

Polloway, E. H., and Cohens, S. B. (1981). Written language for mildly handicapped student. *Focus on Exceptional Children, 14,* 3.

Polloway, E. H., and Patton, J. R. (1996). Strategies for teaching learners with special needs (6th ed.). Columbus, Ohio: Merrill.

Polloway, P. T., and Hallahan, D. P. (1996). Practical questions about collaboration between general and special educators. In E. L. Meyer, G. A. Vergasar, and R. J. Whelan (eds.), *Strategies for teaching exceptional learners in inclusive settings.* Denver: Love Publishing Co. (pp. 401–18).

Ponte, C. R., Zins, J. E., and Graden, J. L. (1988). Implementing a consolidation-based service delivery system to decrease referrals for special education. A case study of organizational considerations. *School Psychology Review, 17,* 89–100.

Poteet, J. A., Choate, J. S., and Stewart, S. C. (1993). Performance assessment and special education: Practices and prospects. *Focus on Exceptional Children.* Oct., 1–13.

Poteet, J., Choote, J. S., and Stewart, S. C. (1996). Performance assessment and special education: Practices and prospects. In E. L. Meyer, G. A. Vergasor, and R. J. Whelan (eds.), *Strategies for teaching exceptional children in inclusive settings.* (pp. 209–42). Denver: Love Publishing Co.

Pugach, M. C., and Johnson, L. J. (1988). Rethinking the relationship between consultation and collaborative problem-solving. *Focus on Exceptional Children, 21,* 1–8.

———. (1989). Preferred interventions: Progress, problems, and challenges. *Exceptional Children, 56,* 217–26.

Pugach, M. C., and Palinscar, A. S. (1995). Creating false impressions. *Phi Delta Kappa,* June, p. 821.

Reeve, P. T., and Hallahan, D. P. (1994). Practical questions and answers about collaboration between general and regular educators. *Focus on Exceptional Children, 26,* (7), 1–10.

Research for Better Schools (1986). *Special educational: Views from America's cities.* Philadelphia: Author.

Reynolds, M. C., and Birch, J. W. (1977). *Teaching exceptional children in America's schools.* Reston, VA: C.E.C. Publications.

Reynolds, M. C., Wang, M. C., and Walberg, H. J. (1987). The necessary restricting of special regular education. *Exceptional Children, 53,* 391–98.

Salend, S. J., and Taylor, L. (1993). Working unit families: A cross-cultural perspective. *Remedial and Special Education, 14,* (5), 25–32, 39.

Salvia, J., and Ysseldyke, J. E. (1995). Assessment in special and remedial education, (5 ed.). Boston, MA: Houghton Mifflin.

Samuda, R. J., Kong, S. L., Cummins, J., Pascual-Leone, J., and Lewis, J. (1989). *Assessment and placement of minority students.* Toronto: Intercultural Social Sciences Publications.

Shutte, R., and Hopkins, B. L. (1970). The effects of teacher attention on following instructions in a kindergarten class. *Journal of Applied Behavior Analysis, 3,* 117–22.

Siegal, E., and Gold, R. (1982). *Educating the learning disabled.* New York: Macmillan.

Sileo, T. W., Sileo, A. P., and Prates, M. A. (1996). Parent and professional partnerships in special education: Multicultural considerations. *Intervention in School and Clinic, 31* (3), 145–53.

Silverman, R., Zigmond, N., and Sanzone, J. (1981). Teaching coping skills to adolescents with learning problems. *Focus on Exceptional Children, 13,* February.

Slavin, R. E. (1983). *Cooperative learning.* New York: Longman.

Smith, C. R. (1995). *Learning disabilities: The interaction of learner, task and setting.* Boston: Little Brown, 3rd ed.

Smith, T. E. C., Dowdy, C. A., Polloway, E. A., Blalock, G. E. (1997). *Children and adults with learning disabilities.* Boston: Allyn & Bacon.

Spradley, J. P. (1979). *The ethnographic interview.* New York: Holt, Rinehart and Winston.

Steinberg, J. (1997). Special education practices in New York faulted by U.S. *New York Times*, June 1, pp. 1, 22.

Stephens, T. M., and Cooper, J. O. (1980). The token economy: An affirmative perspective. *Educational Forum*, November, 107–11.

Tate, B. G., and Baroff, G. S. (1966). Aversive control of self-injuries behavior in a psychotic boy. *Behavior and Research and Therapy 4*, 281–87.

Thompson, D. G. (1977). *Writing long-term and short-term objectives: A painless approach.* Champagne, IL: Research Press.

Thomas, D. R., Becker, W. C., and Armstrong, M. (1968). Production and elimination of descriptive behavior of systematically varying teachers' behavior. *Journal of Applied Behavior Analysis, 1*, 3–45.

Trent, S. C., and Artiles, A. J. (1995). Serving culturally diverse students with emotional or behavioral disorder: Broadenting current perspectives. In J. M. Kauffman, J. W. Lloyd, D. P. Hallahan, and T. A. Astuto (eds.), *Issues in Educational Placement.* Hillside, NJ: Lawrence Erlbaum Associates.

Tucker, J. (1985). Curriculum-based assessment. An introduction. *Exceptional Children, 52,* (3), 199–204.

Warren, C. (1987). *Special education reform: Prepare all teachers to meet diverse needs.* A report of the Public Education Association.

Wesson, C.L., and King, R. P. (1996). Portfolio assessment and special education students. *Teaching Exceptional Children, 28,* (2), 44–49.

White, M. A. (1975). Natural rates of teacher approval and disapproval in classroom. *Journal of Applied Behavior Analysis, 8,* 367–72.

Will, M. (1986). Educational children with learning problems. A shared responsibility. *Exceptional Children, 52,* 411–15.

Williams, B. F. (1992). Changing demographics: Challenges for educators. *Intervention in School and Clinic, 27,* 157–62.

Willig A. C. (1986). Special education and the culturally and linguistically different child: An overview of issues and challenges. *Reading, Writing and Learning Disabilities, 2,* 161–73.

Ysseldyke, J. E., and Algozzine, B. (1995). *Special education: A practical approach for teachers* (3rd ed.). Boston: Houghton Mifflin.

Zigmond, N., Vallecorsa, A., and Silverman, R. (1983). *Assessment for instructional planning special education.* Englewood Cliffs, NJ: Prentice–Hall.

INDEX